Ernest Alexander Cruikshank

Blockade of Fort George

1813

Ernest Alexander Cruikshank

Blockade of Fort George
1813

ISBN/EAN: 9783337268732

Printed in Europe, USA, Canada, Australia, Japan

Cover: Foto ©ninafisch / pixelio.de

More available books at **www.hansebooks.com**

"Ducit Amor Patriae."

NIAGARA HISTORICAL SOCIETY,

No. 3

BLOCKADE OF

FORT GEORGE.

1813.

BY

ERNEST CRUIKSHANK,

MAJOR 44TH LINCOLN AND WELLAND BATTALION,

AUTHOR OF

"THE STORY OF BUTLER'S RANGERS," "THE BATTLE OF LUNDY'S LANE," &c., &c., &c.

WELLAND TRIBUNE PRESSES

PREFACE.

IT has long been desired that the history of the seven months' occupation of Niagara, by the Americans, till now an unwritten chapter in our history, might be given to the public : and we rejoice that the story is now to be told by one who is at once so able and so well informed. and who has made the history of this period and this locality the study of his life. Major Cruikshank needs no introduction to those interested in the history of Canada, and who are already familiar with the close research, patient investigation and judicial impartiality which mark his historical papers. " The Blockade of Fort George" is the sequel to pamphlet No. 1 of the Society, " The Taking of Fort George," and brings the story down to the burning of the town in December, 1813.

The Niagara Historical Society, in sending out this third pamphlet, desires to do its share in proving the fact, so long denied, that Canada has indeed a noble history, and would hope that the same favor granted to its other publications may be accorded to this.

BRITISH FORT AT NIAGARA

From Herriot's Travels, 1806.

For the engraving of Fort George we are indebted to the kindness of Mr. Bain, Librarian, Public Library, Toronto, who has allowed the copper-plate engraving in Herriot's Travels, 1806, to be copied. This interesting picture, which we have been so fortunate as to obtain, confirms and clears up several disputed points. The different buildings forming Navy Hall are seen below Fort George; also a large building on the hill, supposed to have been the first Butler's Barracks, as on this spot are still found Butler's Rangers' buttons. St. Mark's Church is plainly visible, and the large building to the right may have been the Court House, as tradition points to that spot. The view is from near Youngstown and shows part of the stockade of Fort Niagara

J. C.

The Battle of Stoney Creek and the Blockade of Fort George.

On the afternoon of the 27th of May, 1813, the left wing of the weak division commanded by Brigadier-General Vincent was driven from its position at Niagara with severe loss, both of men and munitions of war, and began its retreat by way of St. Davids and DeCew's Falls. Colonel Robert Nichol, the Quartermaster-General of Militia, relates that General Vincent at first intended to retire to Fort Erie, in the hope of maintaining himself there until he could be joined by Colonel Procter's division from the Detroit River, and that only his own strong objections, supported by Lieut.-Colonel Harvey and Captain Milnes of the Governor-General's staff, prevented him from adopting that very hazardous course and induced him to retreat upon Burlington Heights instead.

The numerous small detachments posted at the batteries along the river, between Queenston and Chippawa, dismantled their works and joined the retreating column in the course of the afternoon, and a halt was made for the night at the Beaver Dams, where a small magazine of ammunition and provisions had been formed several days before, in anticipation of this emergency. Before morning Lieut.-Colonel Cecil Bisshopp came in with the greater part of the force which had been watching the river and lake shore between Chippawa and Point Abino, and two companies of the 8th Regiment, accompanied by a few officers and seamen of the Royal Navy under Captain R. H. Barclay on the way to join the Lake Erie squadron, marched across the country from Twenty-Mile Creek, where they had arrived in boats from Burlington the preceding afternoon en route for Fort George.

All the heavy artillery mounted on the fortifications and a great proportion of the bulkiest stores of the army were necessarily destroyed or abandoned, and the militia residing on the south side of the Chippawa were instructed to disband.

It soon appeared that there was little danger of molestation from pursuit. The American army was too much exhausted by the efforts of the day to follow far. General Dearborn and his second in command, General Lewis, even seem to have been in some doubt as to the direction of Vincent's retreat. A party of light infantry had advanced cautiously along the Queenston road for two or three miles when it was peremptorily recalled from fear of an ambuscade. Several of their armed vessels then ascended the river to cover the passage of Colonel Burn with a regiment of dragoons and a body of heavy artillery from the Five Mile Meadows. These troops crossed several hours too late to intercept Vincent's retreat as had been projected. Yet on the whole the invading army was decidedly elated by its partial success, gained with trifling loss, and it was triumphantly announced that "the American flag now proudly waves over the Pandora's box of the frontiers."

Before night came Dearborn was again quite prostrated by illness and fatigue, and retired to his quarters at Fort Niagara, leaving orders for General Lewis to continue the pursuit at daybreak next morning in the direction of the Beaver Dams, where it was then reported that the British intended to make a stand. The village and neighboring farm houses were found to be almost entirely deserted. Many of the inhabitants had fled to the hamlet at the mouth of the Twelve-Mile Creek, already sometimes known as St. Catharines, whither several of the wounded militia men from the battle-field were also conveyed by their sorrowing friends. Most of the houses near the fort had been riddled with cannon-shot during the tremendous bombardment of the last two days, and were scarcely habitable.

The invaders soon obtained from their sympathizers a very accurate estimate of the force opposed to them, but remained in uncertainty as to its movements. General Lewis, with the brigades of Chandler and Winder, besides some dragoons and riflemen, moved in pursuit as instructed, but failed to reach Queenston until afternoon. He then ascertained that a party of the Lincoln Militia, led by Lieut.-Colonel Thomas Clark, had re-occupied that place during the morning and destroyed or concealed all the stores abandoned there the day before. Finding comfortable quarters for the night at Queenston, easy-going General Lewis halted there for the night with Winder's brigade, but directed Chandler to advance to St. Davids. Chandler occupied St. Davids just before dark and encamped there.

During the day considerable numbers of the Lincoln Militia had joined General Vincent in expectation of a battle, but as he feared that his opponent might re-embark his troops in the fleet and cut his line of communication by taking possession of Burlington before he could arrive, it was announced that all who desired were at liberty to return to their homes. Every wagon that could be found was instantly impressed to remove the stores, and the retreat was continued to the Forty-Mile Creek, thirty-one miles from Niagara. The remainder of the militia, with the exception of sixty picked men who were determined to follow the fortunes of the army, were there disbanded and advised to remain quietly at their homes until their services were again required.

Lieut.-Colonel J. P. Preston of the 12th United States Infantry crossed the river during the day from Black Rock with about 600 men, and took possession of the dismantled works at Fort Erie without opposition. Before night it was definitely ascertained that Vincent was retiring towards the head of the lake, and Dearborn then determined to recall Lewis and embark his division in the hope of intercepting him at Burlington. Chauncey readily agreed to this proposition, Lewis had returned to Fort George on the afternoon of the 29th, and preparations for the movement were far advanced, when a messenger arrived from Sackett's Harbor with the alarming intelligence that the British squadron had appeared on the lake and was menacing that port, where all their naval stores were collected and a large new ship of war lay on the stocks nearly ready for launching. In fact the result of the disastrous bombardment of Fort George had become known little more than twenty-four hours later to the Governor-General of Canada at Kingston, and he promptly determined to put the greater part of the garrison on board such of the vessels in the harbor as had been pronounced ready for service, and attempt a diversion in favor of the hardly pressed Vincent by a sudden counter-stroke at the American base of operations. This well-planned movement was only partially successful, but it actually put an end to the proposed expedition by water against Burlington, gave Vincent time to refresh his wearied men, and secured the command of the lake for two months to come. Chauncey decided that he must return to the protection of Sackett's Harbor without delay, yet the 30th was wholly consumed in the embarkation of Macomb's regiment of artillery, and he did not sail until the afternoon of the next day.

Vincent halted for two days at the Forty-Mile Creek, during which his scouts and spies seem to have kept him well informed of the movements of the enemy, although they estimated his force at ten thousand when it probably did not exceed seven. His apprehensions as to the disaffection of many of the inhabitants had certainly not abated, for in a letter of the 29th he wrote:—

"I cannot conceal from Your Excellency my conviction that, unless some disaster attends their progress, that force will daily increase. My sentiments regarding the militia are already known, and it will not be supposed that their attachment to our cause can be very steady under the peculiar complexion of the present times."

On that day Captain Merritt, with a party of the Provincial Dragoons, had patroled the lake road as far as St. Catharines without meeting the enemy, but learned that some of their mounted men had been seen near DeCew's. A wounded militia officer, who had been paroled by them, informed him of their movement upon Queenston and affirmed his belief that they were preparing to pursue in force. He was at once sent on to warn General Vincent, while the dragoons were posted so as to observe all the approaches to the camp. At night Merritt retired to the Twenty, where he was overtaken by Major Pinkney and two other American officers bearing a flag of truce, ostensibly for the purpose of communicating an unimportant message from General Dearborn that the families of the officers and soldiers left behind at Niagara would be permitted to go to York or Kingston if Vincent would send a vessel to receive them. Their real mission was, of course, to obtain information to facilitate the pursuit.

On the last day of May Vincent resumed his march, and at night took up a very strong position on Beaseley's farm at Burlington Heights, where he then proposed making a stand until he received reinforcements or instructions to retire further. Flanked on one side by the lake and on the other by a broad and impassable marsh, his encampment could only be approached in front by a narrow neck of land blocked by a field work, behind which he planted the whole of his artillery. So important did he consider the occupation of this position that he declared "without it he could neither retain possession of the peninsula nor make a safe exit from it."

His last outpost, a party of thirty men that had remained at Fort Erie until the morning of the 28th to keep up a cannonade and destroy the works, joined him before morning, and Vincent then had at his command a compact and efficient body of eighteen hundred officers and men, with eleven guns. A braver and better disciplined force could not have been assembled on the continent. Five companies of the 8th or King's Regiment under Major (afterwards Major-General) James Ogilvie, in spite of appalling losses, both at York and Fort George, still numbered 382 of all ranks. The wing of the 41st mustered 400, but was notably deficient in officers, having only ten for five companies, and but two captains. The battalion of the 49th had been reduced by casualties to 631 officers and men, while the detachment of Royal Artillery (four officers and sixty men) was much too weak to work their guns without assistance from the infantry. The 49th was commanded by Major C. A. Plenderleath and the artillery by Major William Holcroft, well tried and excellent officers. The small detachments of the Royal Newfoundland and Glengarry Regiments had behaved splendidly in the recent action. The militia, including Runchey's colored corps and Merritt's Dragoons, numbered only 131, but these were men of undoubted loyalty and courage, thoroughly acquainted with the country and its inhabitants.

Vincent himself can scarcely be termed a brilliant soldier, but his talents were respectable and he was certainly a man of energy, resolution, and dauntless courage. These qualities had already so strongly impressed the Governor-General that he remarked that General Vincent had "displayed superior talents and ability and a determination worthy of a British soldier." He was then forty-eight years of age and had been thirty years in the army. Promotion had been slow, and long service in the West Indies, followed by a year in a French prison, had seriously injured his health. He had seen war in San Domingo, at the Helder and at Copenhagen in Nelson's great battle.

Lieut.-Colonel John Harvey, Deputy Adjutant-General and principal staff officer to this division, although thirteen years younger than the General, had a far more varied experience of actual warfare. As an ensign in the 80th he had carried the colors of his regiment through the severe campaign of 1794 in Holland. Next year he took part in the ill-starred expedition to Isle Dieu and Quiberon Bay, and in 1796 served at the conquest of the Cape of Good Hope. During the three following years he saw some hard bush-fighting in the interior of Ceylon, and shared in the glory of Abercrombie's expedition to Egypt. Returning to India, he served on the staff of General Dowdeswell during the Mahratta war of 1803-5, under Lord Lake, whose daughter he married. For the past three years he had been Assistant Adjutant-General for the south-eastern district of England. Arriving at Halifax in the winter, when the St. Lawrence was blocked by ice, he determined, without hesitation, to attempt the fatiguing march overland on snow shoes to Quebec, and, being detailed for duty in Upper Canada, he went on at once to Niagara. Great confidence was justly placed in his undoubted ability and experience of war in all its phases.

Lieut.-Colonel Cecil Bisshopp, Inspecting Field Officer, was another officer of more than ordinary talent and promise. The only surviving son of Sir Cecil Bisshopp, Bart., of Parham, Sussex, he had entered the guards at an early age, and as military attache had accompanied Sir John Borlase Warren in his embassy to St. Petersburg. On his return he accompanied his regiment to Spain and served during the entire campaign under Sir John Moore, ending with the memorable battle of Corunna. He acted as a staff officer during the siege of Flushing. Soon after this he was elected member of Parliament for the borough of Newport in the Isle of Wight, but in 1809 he volunteered for service in Portugal, where he acted as aide-de-camp to Sir Arthur Wellesley until he obtained his majority. After war was declared by the United States he received his present appointment, and had commanded the right wing since November, 1812, when he had frustrated General Smyth's attempt at invasion near Fort Erie. "Though heir to an ancient title and a very considerable fortune," says the Gentleman's Magazine of that year. "nothing could damp his military ardor or lessen the zeal which ever stimulated him to the discharge of the duties of his profession. He was humane, generous, noble."

Ogilvie of the 8th, Plenderleath and Dennis of the 49th, the latter of whom had barely recovered from wounds received at Queenston, and Holcroft of the artillery, were all very capable officers. Captain H. B. O. Milnes, aide-de-camp to Sir George Prevost, a very promising young soldier, who was destined to meet his death in an unimportant skirmish a couple of months later, was temporarily attached to this division as a staff-officer.

In his new position Vincent felt tolerably secure for a few days at least, and sent an urgent message for a detachment of the 8th, which he expected to be on its march from Kingston, to hurry forward. At the same time he attempted to relieve the distress of Colonel Procter's division for want of provisions by sending a few trusty officers of the militia to purchase cattle and drive them to Detroit. The military chest was empty, and he was forced to borrow five hundred guineas from Lieut.-Colonel Thomas Clark for this purpose. The departure of the American fleet from Niagara was made known to him the same night, but he supposed at first that York was its destination and expressed the hope that the British squadron would soon be upon the lake to meet it and give him an opportunity of retaking Fort George. Yet at this moment, when he was already calmly proposing to take the offensive, his troops were suffering greatly for want of "shoes, stockings, blankets, tents and shirts"—in fact nearly everything that could contribute to their comfort in the field.

Upon the return of Major Pinkney's flag of truce to the American camp. General Winder was directed to move in pursuit, and on the morning of the 1st of June, he began his march with two companies of artillery, a squadron of dragoons, a detachment of riflemen and the 5th, 13th, 14th, and 16th regiments of United States Infantry. Heavy rains had fallen during the last few days and the roads were deep with mud, but his advance guard, consisting of 400 dragoons, riflemen and light infantry, moved forward that day to the Fifteen Mile Creek, while the main body arrived at St. Catharines. A second flag of truce was sent on to inform General Vincent that twenty-three British prisoners had been placed in close confinement as hostages for the safety of an equal number of

American soldiers of British birth taken at Queenston and sent to England to be tried for treason.

A deserter from Winder's brigade came into Vincent's lines next day and furnished a very accurate statement of his force and its movements. At the time the British general entertained no fears as to the probable result of an attack unless it was made by overwhelming numbers, and described his own troops as being "in great spirits" and "waiting most anxiously for an order to return to Fort George." John Norton had come in with a few Mohawks and declared his firm determination "to exert himself to annoy the enemy, and should he be thwarted in this country in prevailing upon a sufficient number of warriors to second his endeavors," that he would appeal to the Western Indians for support. The remainder of the Grand River Indians had returned to their settlements immediately after the capture of Fort George, and, having driven away their cattle and concealed their families in the woods, were now said to be assembling at a place fourteen miles from Burlington, but it was hinted that they were discreetly holding off through fear of losing their lands if the Americans succeeded.

On the 2d, Winder's light troops drove Merritt's videttes back from the Twenty, and on the following day advanced to the Forty Mile Creek, taking three of his troopers and forcing the remainder to retire behind Stoney Creek quite worn out by fatigue and loss of sleep. General Chandler was then instructed to join Winder, with a third company of artillery, another detachment of rifles and the 9th, 23d and 25th regiments of infantry, and assume command of the whole force. On the evening of the 4th he overtook Winder at the Forty, and advanced next morning with the intention of marching across Burlington Beach and turning Vincent's left flank. At three o'clock, Captain Hindman, who was leading the advance, consisting of three companies of artillery acting as light infantry, Lytle's company of riflemen and Selden's troop of dragoons, came upon the British out-picket commanded by Captain Williams of the 49th. The picket retired through the woods, firing briskly as they went, and finally made a determined stand in and about a saw mill where the main road crossed Stoney Creek. One of Hindman's men having been killed and several wounded in an unsuccessful attempt to dislodge them, General Chandler ordered up the 25th Infantry to support the riflemen, when the British abandoned their position and disappeared in the woods.

Colonel Harvey advanced to support Williams with the light company of the 8th and a few dragoons, but found that the Americans had already abandoned the pursuit and were preparing to encamp. This gave him an excellent opportunity to reconnoitre

their position, of which he made good use. He picked up one or
two prisoners and was joined by a deserter, from whom he obtained
some valuable information. On his return he reported that "the
enemy's camp guards were few and negligent: that his line of
encampment was long and broken: that his artillery was feebly
supported; and that several of his corps were placed too far to the
rear to aid in repelling a blow which might be rapidly struck in
front." A piece of woods extending close to the front of their
encampment would serve at once to mask the advance of an assail-
ing force and to cover its retreat. He warmly advised an attack
that night. Vincent was the more disposed to assent as he had become convinced that his own position was scarcely tenable against
so large a force. "This position, though strong for a large body,"
he wrote, "is far too extensive for me to hope to make any successful stand against the superior force understood to be advancing
against me in three separate points, viz., by the lake, by the centre
road, and by the mountain on my right. The attack, I knew, would
not be delayed: I had neither time nor inclination precipitately
to retreat from my position." He had already for some time been
considering the advisability of an offensive movement if an opportunity offered, for on the 4th he had informed the Adjutant-General: "By a report I have just received from my outposts, an
attack cannot be far distant. As circumstances are at present, I am
determined, *if possible, to be beforehand with them.*" Since writing
that, however, the enemy's force had been nearly doubled and the
chances of failure proportionately increased.

General Chandler, who now commanded the American troops
at Stoney Creek, had been a blacksmith in early life and "the
poorest man in the settlement" where he lived. He became a tavern
keeper and soon grew wealthy. In 1805 he was elected a repre-
sentative in Congress from Massachusetts and served two terms. As
a reward for political activity, he was appointed in the first place a
Major-General in the militia of his own State, and, on the increase
of the regular army at the declaration of war, a Brigadier-General
in the service of the United States. He was then fifty-three years
of age and had not the slightest military education or experience,
and as one of his associates remarked, "the march from the anvil
and the dram shop in the wane of life to the dearest actions of the
tented field is not to be achieved in a single campaign."

Winder, his second in command, had been an able and successful lawyer in Baltimore. Once a warm Federalist, he had lately
changed sides and his defection was at once rewarded by a commission as Lieutenant-Colonel of the 14th United States Infantry,
then being recruited in Maryland. In November, 1812, he had

directed the unsuccessful operations for the passage of the river below Fort Erie and acquitted himself creditably. During the winter he had been summoned to Washington to advise the Cabinet, and was supposed to be intimately acquainted with the plan of campaign. "Colonel Winder is here," says a contemporary letter, "a kind of Secretary of War, and, like Bonaparte, has a room full of maps, plans, &c., &c., enveloped in which you can just see his little head, and of that little head much is expected." His aptitude and ability so strongly impressed even a veteran like Harvey that he declared that he possessed "more talent than all the rest of the Yankee generals put together."

General Chandler asserted in his defence that he told Winder, "if the enemy intended to fight them, he would commence the attack before morning, and with this expectation arrangements were made." It was growing dark when the light troops were recalled. None of his men had eaten during the march, and were then ordered to build fires and cook some distance from the ground it was intended to occupy for the night, the light infantry and 25th regiment in the meadow about 150 yards in front, and the remainder on a high ridge in rear and to the left of the road. About eight hundred men, consisting of the 13th and 14th regiments of infantry and Archer's artillery company, were detached under Colonel Christie to take up a position near the mouth of the creek for the protection of a flotilla of boats conveying the baggage and supplies for the division which was expected to arrive there during the night. It was nearly midnight when the remainder of the force received orders to form their encampment, those in front being instructed to leave their line of fires burning, while the fires on the high ground in rear were to be extinguished. The ground selected for the men to lie on was a piece of level upland, protected in front by a steep descent, along the brow of which ran a stout fence of logs and rails. On either side of this fence a number of trees had been felled years before, but not cleared away, about which thorns and briars had grown up to form an almost impenetrable thicket in some places. The low, level meadows beneath were spongy with long continued rain. "On the left the mountain and woods shut down so close upon the meadow as to render that flank quite secure, and the right was equally protected by a swamp, which approached it in that quarter." Six field guns belonging to Leonard's and Towson's companies were planted on the brow of the upland, to command the main road to Burlington. The 25th regiment was posted on the right of the artillery, the infantry in rear was instructed to move obliquely forward towards the road and fence, and in the event of an attack, the 23rd was to form in rear of the guns with the 16th, 5th and light troops on its left. A squadron of dragoons was encamped on the road behind. The 9th Infantry, being the weakest regiment in the division, was detailed to form the rearguard, nearly a mile away. A strong main guard was mounted at a small church or meeting house, almost half a mile in advance, with an outlying picket on the right of the meadow near the edge of the swamp, and another on the left, close to the base of the mountain. A chain of sentinels was then posted around the entire camp. As these arrangements were made in the dark, it is probable that they were very imperfectly executed. The soldiers were ordered to ground arms, take off knapsacks and lie down on their blankets as they stood in their companies and sections. The artillery horses stood in their harness near the guns.

From a return prepared by Major Johnson, Assistant Adjutant General, it appears that General Chandler's division mustered 2,643 rank and file that morning before marching from Forty Mile Creek. Including the officers and other supernumeraries, its total strength must have slightly exceeded 3000 of all ranks. One hundred and eighty men remained behind on guard or sick, and, eight hundred having been detached to the mouth of the creek, left about two thousand in camp.

The two generals remained together for several hours in Chandler's tent, which was pitched close beside Gage's house, and it was nearly one o'clock when the 25th regiment moved into its position for the night. The men, excited by the events of the day and the near prospect of a battle, were noisy and wakeful. Several times after that the fires on the ridge blazed up or were rekindled, and the orders for their extinction were repeated.

Just before midnight the column detailed for the attack marched out of the lines at Burlington, seven miles distant. It consisted of 280 officers and men of the 8th, under Major Ogilvie, and 424 of the 49th, commanded by Major Plenderleath. Colonel Harvey conducted the force and appears to have directed its operations, but was accompanied by General Vincent and a small staff of volunteers, eager to share in the perils of the enterprise, among whom were Brigade Major J. B. Glegg, Captain P. L. Chambers of the 41st, who had just arrived with despatches from Detroit, and Captains McDouall and Milnes, both aides to the Governor General, lately sent from Kingston on a similar service. Colonel Bisshopp, with the remainder of the division, manned the works at Burlington in readiness to cover the retreat in the event of disaster.

The weather was as favorable as could be well desired for an attack with a small force. A cloudy sky and a light mist rising from the wet ground made the darkness almost impenetrable. Although the mud impeded the march it effectually muffled the sound of their footsteps.

The light companies of the two regiments, led by Captain Munday of the 8th and Lieut. Danford of the 49th, headed the column, followed by the remainder of the 49th in the centre and the 8th in rear. It was nearly three o'clock when the advance came upon the first American outpost. The sentry on the road, being half asleep and quite ignorant of his duties, was taken prisoner without noise, and readily gave every information in his power. Nothing could then be seen of the main guard, but it was soon discovered that they had gone to sleep in the church, where they were surrounded and captured to a man. The remaining sentries "were approached and bayoneted in the quietest manner," and the eager light companies dashed forward among the smouldering camp fires in the meadow, which they supposed were still surrounded by sleeping enemies. To their great surprise they found them absolutely deserted, and halting within their glare hurriedly began to fix flints. The groans of the dying and the rush of the advancing column alarmed some of the surviving sentries, who discharged their arms at random in the darkness, and in an instant the entire camp was aroused.

General Chandler, who had not gone to sleep, instantly mounted his horse and gave orders for the troops next his tent to form for action, which was done in a moment, as they had only to rise to their feet and seize their arms. He then sent an officer to direct General Winder to advance to the fence on the brow of the height with the infantry on the left. From this position the British column could be seen by the light of the fires beneath in the act of deploying to the left, while the American line of battle was quite invisible to them. The American light infantry and 5th and 25th regiments began firing, followed by the artillery. The 49th suffered severely while deploying, and was thrown into great confusion. At this critical moment Major Plenderleath, with the assistance of Sergeant-Major Alexander Fraser, hastily assembled fifteen or twenty men and rushed at the guns, whose position was disclosed by a vivid sheet of flame. Two discharges swept harmlessly over their heads as they climbed the height, and before they could re-load a third time the gunners were bayoneted or flying for their lives. Without hesitation this gallant little band plunged into the midst of the nearest body of infantry, which instantly dispersed, leaving the artillery horses and ammunition waggons in their possession. Plenderleath's timely onset was decisive. The remainder of the 49th came rapidly to his support. The American line was cut in two, four of their guns taken, and the others silenced.

Ogilvie led the 8th against the 5th and 16th United States Infantry forming the left of their line. Lieut. Hooper, commanding one of the companies, was killed in this charge, but the regiment carried the heights, entirely dispersing the 16th and driving the 5th back upon the dragoons.

Meanwhile General Chandler, while riding to the right, had his horse shot under him, and was much stunned and bruised by the fall. Returning on foot towards the artillery, which he noticed had ceased firing, he walked directly into the midst of the 49th. He attempted to conceal himself under a gun carriage, but was ignominiously dragged out by the strong arm of gigantic Sergeant Fraser, to whom he gave up his sword. A few minutes later General Winder was dismounted, and taken prisoner in a very similar manner.

The scattered and bewildered American infantry made several creditable attempts to rally. Wherever they could be seen they were immediately charged and dispersed. Their dragoons mounted and attempted a charge, which ended in riding down some of their own 16th Infantry. Desultory fighting continued in various parts of the field until day began to break, when Harvey found himself in possession of the enemy's camp it is true, but with his small force much scattered and diminished. Officers had lost their commands in the darkness, and wandered blindly about the field seeking them. General Vincent himself had disappeared, and was supposed to have been killed or taken prisoner. Companies had become separated from their battalions, and sections from their companies. His loss in killed and wounded had been severe, particularly among the officers. Major Dennis had received two gunshot wounds and was sorely bruised by the fall of his horse, which had been killed under him. Ensign Drury, who carried the King's color of the 49th, was mortally wounded, but struggled forward until he could give it into the keeping of another officer. Brevet-Major Clerk, Captain Manners, Adjutant Stean of the 49th, Major Ogilvie, Captains Munday and Goldrick, Lieutenants Boyd and Weyland of the 8th, and Fort-Major Taylor, was also among the injured. A large escort had been sent off with the prisoners, and Harvey could not have had five hundred men left fit for duty at this time. He was encumbered by many wounded men, and the enemy, although driven from the field, was not routed, but seemed to be assembling in force to renew the contest. They still had several field-guns, and their cavalry and two or three infantry regiments had taken little or no part in the action. Harvey prudently determined to retreat before they had recovered from their confusion and could discern the weakness of their assailants and bring forward these fresh troops.

Most of the wounded were collected and removed, but several, including Major Clerk and Captain Manners, were too badly hurt to be taken away. Two of the captured guns, after being removed some distance, were abandoned for want of horses to haul them. A brass howitzer, with its limber and tumbril and one iron six-pounder were brought off, with nine captured horses. Besides the two Generals, Major VanDeVenter of their staff, Captain Steel commanding the 16th Regiment, Captain Mills of the 23d, five subalterns and 116 non-commissioned officers and privates were taken prisoners.

The British casualties on this occasion amounted to twenty-three killed, one hundred and thirty-six wounded and fifty-five missing, or rather more than a fourth of the whole number engaged. The 8th lost eighty-three, and the 49th one hundred and thirty of all ranks.

That of their opponents is more difficult to ascertain. No official and detailed return was ever published. One account, which has been frequently repeated, places it at seventeen killed, thirty-eight wounded, and only ninety-nine missing, whereas, one hundred and twenty-five prisoners were certainly brought off. Even this, is greatly at variance with official statements. General Dearborn, in a letter written from Fort George on the evening of the same day, asserted the entire loss did not exceed thirty, and remarked "that by some strange fatality both Generals Chandler and Winder were taken prisoners." Probably he had not then learned the full extent of the disaster. The command devolved upon Colonel Burn of the 2d Dragoons. An extract from his official letter was published, but it contains no statement of loss. Major Smith, who commanded the 25th Infantry, reported that his regiment alone lost forty-two in killed and wounded, and there is no reason to suppose that it suffered more than several others. The 16th, for instance, after losing its commander fell into irretrievable confusion, some of its companies firing on each other. Unofficial accounts frankly admitted a serious reverse.

One letter, printed in *Poulson's American*, published in Philadelphia, dated at Fort George on the 9th of June, relates that "at daybreak we could not muster more than sixty of our regiment, the remainder being killed, wounded or prisoners. Of the fine battalion of artillery not more than seventy were left. Captain Biddle's company only mustered twenty men. The British carried off two pieces of cannon and two or three hundred prisoners. We took about sixty prisoners."

Another private letter from Buffalo, which found its way into the columns of the *Boston Messenger*, gives this version of the affair: "We were surprised at 2.30 a. m., and lost three captains, one assistant quartermaster-general and three hundred and fifty rank and file. We took about fifty prisoners in the woods, after the action. Two of the regiments kept up their fire until daylight, when the 16th, under Captain McChesney, discovered the British removing the cannon and re-captured two pieces."

Christie's detachment from the mouth of the creek arrived on the field soon after Harvey retreated, and the camp was re-occupied. Burn instantly sent a message to inform General Dearborn of the capture of the two generals and convened a council of the principal officers, which determined to retire to the Forty Mile Creek without waiting for orders from headquarters. A quantity of baggage and provisions was destroyed, and the retreat began shortly before noon.

On the other hand, General Vincent's mysterious disappearance caused some confusion in the British camp. The command devolved on Lieut.-Colonel Bisshopp. Captain McDouall produced a letter from the Governor General to Vincent, authorizing him to retreat to Kingston if he considered his position untenable, but instructing him in that event to send the remainder of the 41st and detachments of the Glengarry and Newfoundland regiments to reinforce the Right Division at Detroit. As the full effect of the attack was still unknown, Bisshopp determined to call a council of war to decide what course to pursue, and Captain Merritt rode back to the field of battle to look for their missing general. His search was fruitless, but he made two prisoners, single-handed, and discovered that the enemy was panic-stricken and preparing to retreat. Before the council could assemble, Vincent returned to the lines without his horse and hat. Having been dismounted and separated from his staff in the conflict, he was obliged to take shelter in the woods, where he lay concealed for several hours until he found an opportunity to escape. Instead of retreating, a strong detachment was pushed forward to Stoney Creek, and an hour or two later Captain Milnes was on his way to Kingston with the prisoners and Colonel Harvey's official account of the action.

When Colonel Burn's messenger arrived at Fort George, General Dearborn instantly instructed Major-General Morgan Lewis to join the division at Stoney Creek with the 6th United States Infantry, take command and bring the enemy to action at once. Brigadier-Generals Boyd and Swartwout were ordered to accompany him as brigade commanders. Before they were ready to start, it began to rain and Lewis postponed his own departure until morning. According to General Porter, "he could not go sixteen miles to fight the enemy, not because his force was too small, but because he had not wagons to carry tents and camp kettles for his army. His own baggage moves in two stately wagons—one drawn by two, the other by four horses, carrying the various furniture of a Secretary of State's office, a lady's dressing chamber, an alderman's dining room and the contents of a grocer's shop." In fact, Lewis appears to have been an American counterpart of the Austrian General Mack.

Yet next day, when it was known that Burn had decided to retreat, he advanced so rapidly that he arrived at the camp at Forty Mile Creek at five o'clock in the afternoon. On the road he was overtaken, first by a message from General Dearborn to announce that several vessels had appeared off the mouth of the Niagara, steering towards the head of the lake, which were supposed to belong to the British squadron, directing him to return with his entire division as soon as possible: and then by a second, stating that it was possible that the vessels in sight were part of the American fleet, and that a few hours delay would enable him to ascertain the fact and to act accordingly.

Lewis found Burn encamped on the narrow plain between the lake and mountain. His men were still much dispirited. "I can scarce believe," Colonel Miller of the 6th wrote to his wife, "that you could have been more glad to see me than that army was." An hour later several British warships came in sight, and although when night fell they had not approached the shore very closely, the American General gave orders for his men to lie upon their arms in expectation of another nocturnal visit.

On the 3d of June, Sir George Prevost having returned to Kingston from his late expedition, received Vincent's despatch announcing the fall of Fort George and his retreat towards Burlington. At the same time he knew that the American fleet had returned to Sackett's Harbor the day before. Major Thomas Evans was directed to embark at once with five companies of the 8th Regiment, reduced by casualties to 200 rank and file. Two hundred and fifty men of the Royal Newfoundland had been already sent on board to act as marines, and before night Sir James Yeo left the harbor with a squadron consisting of his flagship, the *Wolfe*, of 23 guns and 200 men, the *Royal George* of 21 guns and 175 men, the brig *Melville* of 14 guns and 100 men, the schooners *Moira*, 14 guns and 100 men, *Sidney Smith*, 12 guns and 80 men, and *Beresford*, of 8 guns and 70 men, besides several light gun-boats.

On the morning of the 7th he appeared off the mouth of the Niagara and sent his light vessels close into the shore to reconnoitre. To the interested spectators in the American lines the vessels seemed at one time to be approaching the mouth of the river, and at another to be standing towards the head of the lake. Before night they were seen to stand away in a north-westerly direction. General Dearborn's hopes that the vessels in sight might be some of his own were dispelled by a letter from Chauncey, informing him that he did not expect to leave Sackett's Harbor until the end of the month, and he became much alarmed in consequence. A third message was despatched in all haste, to inform General Lewis that he suspected that an attack was contemplated on his camp, as two small schooners had been engaged for three or four hours in the minute examination of the shore, and he feared they might take on board additional troops at the head of the lake and land them there before he could return. He was instructed to send back the dragoons and about eight hundred infantry "with all possible despatch," and follow with the remainder of the division "as soon as practicable." He was particularly cautioned to secure the boats conveying the baggage against capture. The entire force at Fort George was kept under arms all night. At two o'clock in the morning several shots were fired by the picquets on the lake shore ; the alarm was beaten and every preparation made to resist an assault, when it was ascertained that the firing had been directed at some of their own boats returning from the Forty Mile Creek with the wounded and some prisoners taken at the Stoney Creek fight.

Yeo had received orders to land the troops as near York as possible. Some time during the morning of the 7th, Major Evans and Lieut. Finch of the 8th were put on shore by one of the smaller vessels and walked to the town, where they learned the result of the late action, and that General Vincent was said to be pursuing the enemy. Evans returned on board at once to urge the Commodore to menace the American encampment while he sent on Finch by land to assure Vincent of the co-operation of the squadron.

At daybreak General Lewis discovered several of the British vessels abreast of his camp and not more than a mile from shore. He instantly began to strike his tents and prepare for a retreat. There was a dead calm and the larger vessels were consequently prevented from approaching closer, but the schooner *Beresford*, Captain Francis Spilsbury, was towed by the boats of the squadron within gun-shot and began firing. She was soon joined by several gun-boats commanded by Lieut. Charles Anthony of the *Wolfe*. About the same time a small party of Indians appeared on the brow of the heights overlooking the encampment, and by their whoops and desultory musketry caused some confusion. The artillery companies of Towson and Archer replied to the *Beresford* from four field-guns, using shot heated in a field furnace hastily constructed for the purpose. After a short and absolutely harmless cannonade, the British vessels retired out of range and the whole squadron bore away towards the head of the lake. The Indians retreated on the approach of a party of light infantry, led by Lieut. Eldridge, Adjutant of the 13th Regiment, who was destined to meet his death at their hands a month later. Just at this moment, about six o'clock a. m., General Dearborn's orders to return to Fort George were delivered to General Lewis. Arrangements for the retreat were conducted with much haste and confusion. Tents and camp kettles were abandoned. Part of the baggage was loaded on the boats, which were then allowed to put off without a sufficient escort. At ten o'clock Lewis began his march, harassed on flank and rear by the Indians and militia, which soon assembled in considerable numbers.

Upon Yeo's arrival at Burlington, Vincent had already given orders for the disembarkation of the 8th when a messenger arrived with information that the enemy were retreating. These were promptly countermanded, and the squadron sailed in pursuit, while Major Dennis, with the grenadier company of the 49th, a strong company of the 41st and two 3-pounder field-pieces, was directed to advance by land. It was then four o'clock in the afternoon, and as Lewis had easily six hours start the prospect of overtaking him must have seemed slight at the time, but, favored by a steady though moderate breeze which had just sprung up, the squadron made such a rapid run that in three hours the troops were landed at the Forty-Mile Creek and were in possession of the American camp. Many tents had been left standing and there were undoubted signs of panic in the arms and baggage abandoned along the line of retreat. The *Beresford* and other light vessels went in chase of the flotilla of boats which took the place of a baggage train to the retiring column, and were rapidly overhauling them when they were run ashore and abandoned by their crews. Twenty large *bateaux* containing the hospital stores, provisions, and remaining baggage of General Chandler's division were taken or destroyed. Major Dennis was immediately directed to advance to the Twenty with his command and push forward the dragoons and Indians within sight of the enemy's outposts at Fort George. Lewis, however, continued his retreat with such rapidity that he arrived at Niagara next day and Dennis was unable to overtake even the rear guard, although his movement was not without some important results.

"Many prisoners were taken," wrote Major Evans, "the spirit of the loyal part of the country aroused, the little remaining baggage of the enemy destroyed, his panic increased and confirmed, and, which is of the utmost consequence, certain information obtained of all his movements. On the evening of the 9th the enemy set fire to and abandoned Fort Erie, withdrew his force from Chippawa and Queenston, concentrating them at Fort George, and hastily began throwing up field-works, either there to defend himself or cross the river by means of boats, which he holds in a constant state of readiness, according to circumstances."

During the three days occupied by this pursuit, the 8th, 9th and 10th of June, eighty prisoners were captured, and 500 tents, 200 camp kettles, 150 stand of arms and a great quantity of baggage taken or destroyed. The total loss of the American army in the battle and the retreat must have been nearly five hundred men. A contemporary newspaper, the *Buffalo Gazette*, estimated that half of that number had been made prisoners.

Vincent then felt so certain of his ability to cope with the invaders in the field that he determined to send the remainder of the 41st Regiment to Procter, who was clamoring for reinforcements, and on the 10th moved his headquarters to the Forty.

"The principal objects," said Harvey in a letter to Colonel Baynes, " General Vincent has had in making a forward movement with the greatest part of the troops to this place, are to communicate with and give every support and assistance in his power to Sir James Yeo and the fleet : to be at hand to take advantage of the success which we sanguinely anticipate from his approaching encounter with Commodore Chauncey : to give encouragement to the militia and yeomanry of the country, who are everywhere rising upon the fugitive Americans and making them prisoners, and withholding all supplies from them : and lastly, (and perhaps *chiefly*,) for the purpose of sparing the resources of the country in our rear and drawing the supplies of this army as long as possible from the country immediately in the enemy's vicinity. Our position here secures all these important objects, and so long as our fleet is triumphant it is a secure one. Should any disaster (which God forbid) befall that, we have no longer any business *here*, or in this part of *Canada.*"

Learning on the 14th that Major De Haren had marched from Kingston five or six days before with a reinforcement of four hundred regular infantry for his division, and nearly as many Indians from Lower Canada, he resolved to wait for his arrival before advancing further. He then intended to move his headquarters to the Twenty and push forward the whole body of light troops to annoy the enemy, " whose fears were said to be as strong as ever." To accomplish this more effectually he requested General Procter to send him a body of the Western Indians, and promised in return, on their arrival, to detach the rest of the 41st Regiment to his assistance.

On the same day the Governor General issued a proclamation from Kingston in reply to Lieut.-Colonel Preston's singular manifesto of the 30th May, in which he called upon "all the loyal and well-disposed in this Province, who are not under the immediate control or within the power of the enemy, to use every possible effort in repelling the foe and driving him from our soil, assuring them that they will be powerfully aided by the reinforcements daily arriving at this post and pressing on to their support."

The evacuation and destruction of Fort Erie were actually accomplished in compliance with instructions received by General Dearborn from the Secretary of War, who wrote to him that in event of the capture of both Fort Erie and Fort George he was to select which of these was to be held as a military post, where he would concentrate his whole force, while all other forts and redoubts were to be dismantled and demolished and all "Indian establishments" destroyed. The unforeseen appearance of the British squadron, combined with Chandler's reverse, caused him to obey in great haste, and abandon everything that lay outside of the picquet line which he had drawn around Niagara and Fort George. Preston's promise of protection was ignored, and such of the inhabitants as had shown a disposition to actively assist the invaders found themselves compelled either to fly from the Province altogether or take refuge in the American camp.

Up to this time General Dearborn had shown a marked inclination to treat all classes of the population with justice and lenity. Several wounded officers and privates belonging to the militia who had been taken prisoners were permitted to return to their homes on parole. He called a meeting of the magistrates, twelve of whom attended, and directed them to continue the exercise of their powers, and several minor offences were punished by them during the first days of the American occupation. Colonel Preston's proclamation, distributed from Fort Erie on the 30th May, declared that as he found the people in the vicinity "anxious to obtain special protections" all who "would come forward and voluntarily enroll their names with him and claim the protection of the United States shall have their property and personal rights secured to them inviolate." At the same time he "solemnly warned those who may obstinately continue inimical that they are bringing on themselves the most rigorous and disastrous consequences, as they will be pursued and treated with that spirit of retaliation which the treatment of the American prisoners in the hands of the British so justly inspires."

The disaffected, the timorous, and apathetic, hastened to comply with his demand, and avert danger of arrest. A letter from the

American camp, dated on the 5th of June, relates that " many persons have come in from distant parts since our arrival and been paroled. Several of them reside on the banks of the Grand River, to the middle and lower parts of which most of the Indians have retired, dreading the reward of their cruelty."

In this way the names of 507 persons were obtained to a list of paroled militiamen, which are generally represented as having been made prisoners in the battle of the 27th May, although very few of them had even borne arms at any time.

General Dearborn undoubtedly believed that he was carrying out the instructions given to him by the Secretary of War in April, just before the attack upon York, when he said, "As regards the course of conduct to be pursued with regard to the inhabitants of Canada the laws of war must govern. Persons behaving peaceably may be protected, but all must be disarmed and the militia paroled. Any persons made prisoners, either of regulars or militia actually armed, must be sent within our limits."

On the 5th of May the small village of Havre de Grace, in Maryland, a rather important station on the main post-road between Philadelphia and the national capital, was partially destroyed in an attack by the boats of a British squadron. This caused much alarm and exasperation in that part of the country, and with this event fresh in his mind the Secretary wrote that: "If the enemy still adheres to the barbarism of attacking and burning defenceless towns on our sea coast, and of employing savage auxiliaries to butcher women and children on our land frontier, our better and more humane principles will yield to the necessity of the case, and instead of them a rigid and inflexible retaliation must be substituted."

Early in June this was followed by a letter, dated on the 26th May, in which the Secretary announced that "owing to embarrassments thrown in the way of exchange by Sir George Prevost and Sir J. B. Warren, make these rules indispensable : 1st. All British officers and men, whether regulars or militia, are to be removed to some place of confinement in the United States. 2d. All male inhabitants of Canada subject to the militia law are to be considered as prisoners and removed as such."

General Dearborn was so reluctant to enforce these harsh instructions that he not only deferred doing so for several days, but warmly remonstrated. "On taking possession of this place," he wrote to the Secretary of War on the 8th of June, " the inhabitants came in in numbers and gave their paroles. I have promised them protection. A large proportion are friendly to the United States, and fixed in their hatred to the Government of Great

Britain. If they should be made prisoners of war and taken from their families it would have a most unfavorable effect on our military operations in the provinces. The whole country would be driven to a state of desperation, and satisfy them beyond doubt that we had no intention of holding the provinces. The same effect would be produced on the Indians, who are now principally quiet for fear of losing their valuable tract of land on Grand River. I had authorized the civil magistrates to continue in the due exercise of their functions, and cannot with propriety revoke this authority, unless specially directed."

The spontaneous rising of the militia against the invaders in the next few days appears to have convinced Dearborn that he had quite misjudged the feelings of the people and removed his scruples. A number of militia officers and others living within reach were seized and deported to Fort Niagara.

"The dragoons and riflemen," says a private letter dated at Newark on the 13th, "are out every day in scouting parties, and seldom return without prisoners. The day before yesterday they brought in fourteen of the militia who had been paroled and were caught with arms. One of these fellows confessed he had assisted in taking twenty-three of our men when the army moved down from the Forty-Mile Creek. With this fellow it will go hard, and I hope there will be a more vigorous course pursued with the inhabitants who are opposed to our cause. This class are principally Scots and Orangemen, and many of them obtain all the information they can and forward it to the enemy."

A correspondent of the *National Advocate* gave this account of the arrest of Captain Jacob A. Ball of the Lincoln Militia, who is described as "an active and cruel commander of Indians:"

"When the party arrived at Six-Mile Creek, Sergeant James Rouse volunteered with two dragoons, and proceeding to the Short Hills discovered the house where Ball was supposed to be, at nine o'clock in the evening. In order to reach the place they were compelled to pass within half a mile of a British picquet guard. On entering the house, Rouse was told that Ball was not there, but he fired his pistol through a door he could not break open, when Ball opened it and surrendered himself with his guard, five in number. They were all placed on horses and carried eighteen miles through the enemy's country to Fort George."

A memorandum by Captain Ball states that he was taken prisoner on the 11th of June at the Ten-Mile Creek, while on command from Burlington to ascertain the position of the enemy at Fort George and vicinity.

On the 19th and two following days, about one hundred persons were suddenly arrested in and about Niagara, among whom were nearly all the best known and most respected of the inhabitants.

A letter dated at "Flamboro', U. C.," June 20th, published in a Montreal newspaper, observes that "plunder is the order of the day among the Americans, and the personal liberty of the inhabitants is taken away from them. Several disaffected persons have joined the enemy - among them the late editor of the *Guardian*. Many of the inhabitants have been sent as prisoners to the United States. Among them Messrs. Edwards, Muirhead, Dickson, Symington, Rev.'d Mr. Addison, Powell, Heron, Baldwin, Clench, James Ball, De-Cew, John Crooks, Lawe, two Kerrs, and McEwen—the last four suffering from wounds received at Fort George." A list of some of the prisoners made by William Dickson, one of their number, in the following January, contains the names of Haggai Skinner, "a farmer 64 years of age"; Joseph Doan, "farmer;" John Ramsay, "a boy of Stamford," and John McFarland, "boat builder," all of whom were detained until December, 1813, in close confinement.*

A letter from Newark dated on the 22d June and published in *Poulson's American* of Philadelphia relates that "the most conspicuous and violent of the British partisans are taken up and sent over to the United States. At the solicitation of the inhabitants who are friendly to our cause, the General has agreed to introduce a a few Indians to combat those of the enemy. In desultory warfare our men seldom gain much, as the enemy is best acquainted with the paths, by-roads, and country in general."

Commenting on the impolicy of this line of conduct in the light of subsequent events six months later, when the American frontier had been laid waste by Drummond's avenging army, the *Manlis Times*, a New York newspaper, remarked: "After Fort George was taken by our troops a system of plunder and outrage was adopted and commenced to an extent almost unequalled in the annals of French warfare. Citizens, while peaceably attending to their business, were seized and sent across the river, and almost at the same time their property was destroyed. Those who were paroled and promised protection, on suspicion of their possessing moveable property were arrested and their property pillaged. The notorious traitor, Willcocks, was commissioned to raise a body of marauders expressly to plunder, burn, and destroy."

The unwisdom of this system was soon made evident by the

* Capts. McEwen, DeCoe (born in New Jersey), Lorimier, Lieuts. Williams (born in Long Island), Humberlin (born in Philadelphia), Stewart, Luke, Duval and Lamont, Ensigns Myers and Kerr, Midshipman Lawe, Sailing-Masters Campbell and Barwis, Seamen Rogers, Byles, and Wood escaped from prison in Philadelphia on April 20th by sawing off the bars of their prison and letting themselves down by blankets. Ensigns Myers and Kerr and five others have been taken.
Salem Gazette, April 29th, 1814.

increased activity of the militia, who seldom permitted a patrol or foraging party to advance very far from the lines without being attacked.

On the tenth of June the Americans scored the solitary advantage to be derived from their temporary occupation of Fort Erie. This was the release of five armed vessels which had been detained at the navy yard at Black Rock by the batteries across the river. Four hundred men and many yoke of oxen were employed for six days in towing them up the rapids, and they set sail for Erie, heavily laden with stores of all kinds necessary for the equipment of the two ships building there. This was an object of supreme importance, for by means of these vessels the Americans gained control of Lake Erie and eventually drove Procter from the Detroit frontier.

On the same day a cavalry patrol guided by Totman, a disaffected inhabitant, chased Captain Merritt away from the Ten and captured four of his dragoons. They did not attempt to maintain the position, and Merritt re-occupied it next morning and carefully examined the roads leading to Fort George without meeting an enemy. On the 12th, however, his party was surprised while resting during the heat of the day by a numerous body of dragoons, and only escaped through the coolness and presence of mind of his only sentry. This trooper, whose name is not recorded, after retiring rapidly to the summit of a rise on the road, halted, wheeled about, and shouted loudly to an imaginary party in their rear to come on, which caused his pursuers to pause and enabled his comrades to assemble and mount. Merritt rode off barely in time to elude a second detachment of the enemy, which had taken a circuit by way of De Cew's Falls to cut off his retreat. One of their scouts, misled by their blue uniforms, rode into the midst of his men and gave them important information before he was undeceived and made prisoner.

It was then made evident that if a small force of active light infantry was detailed to act with the Provincial Dragoons they would be enabled to maintain their ground and perform scouting duty with more effect. James FitzGibbon, Adjutant of the 49th Regiment, an officer of great enterprise and address as well as uncommon physical strength, was selected to command a company of volunteers from the regular troops for this purpose. In three days fifty picked men were equipped, with whom he advanced on the 16th to De-Cew's stone house on the crest of the mountain, at the junction of two important roads, where he established his headquarters and pushed forward his pickets beyond the Ten Mile Creek.

Nearly at the same time General Dearborn resorted to a similar expedient. Finding himself at a marked disadvantage for want of a body of men intimately acquainted with the country and qualified to act as scouts and guides, he authorized the formation of a battalion of mounted riflemen from among the refugees that were daily seeking shelter in his lines. Joseph Willcocks, the former editor of a local newspaper, and even then a member of the Assembly of the Province for one of the divisions of the County of Lincoln, was nominated as Lieutenant Colonel and Benajah Mallory, member of the Assembly for Middlesex, as major of this corps. Markle, Totman and other noted refugees were also rewarded by commissions. The services of another troop of volunteer mounted infantry, organized by Dr. Cyrenius Chapin of Buffalo, then sheriff of Niagara County, for the purpose, as it was stated, "of clearing the frontier of persons inimical to the United States," were also accepted and Chapin was ordered to join the army at Fort George. On the 16th he crossed the river at Black Rock with about fifty men. Two days were employed in scouring the country between Fort Erie and Chippawa, and on the 19th he marched into camp, his men loaded with plunder and followed by the execrations of the outraged inhabitants.

Meanwhile Sir James Yeo had been actively engaged in intercepting supplies destined for Dearborn's army, which was now entirely dependent on transport by water from various magazines along the south shore of the lake. He took on board sixty volunteers from the 8th to act as additional marines, and on the 12th sailed from Forty Mile Creek in search of the enemy. Colonel Harvey relates that he was " fully impressed with the necessity of having a *commanding* breeze before he makes his attack. In a light one or calm, the enemy's flotilla of small vessels would have an incalculable advantage."

In the evening he chased two schooners loaded with hospital stores and provisions into the Eighteen Mile Creek, out of which they were brought by the boats of the squadron just as a body of troops marched up from Fort Niagara for their protection. Yeo then continued his course eastward, looking into all the bays and creeks along the American shore. Two other schooners and several supply boats, bound from Oswego to Niagara, fell into his hands during the next two days, and on the 15th a landing was effected at the mouth of the Genesee, where a large boat loaded with 1200 bushels of corn was taken, and 450 barrels of provisions removed from a public storehouse. On the 16th he anchored in Kingston harbor, barely long enough to take on board the grenadiers and one battalion company of the Royal Scots, which had arrived from Montreal during his absence, and sailed at once for Oswego. Discovering nothing at that place to justify a descent, he proceeded westward along the south shore of the lake as far as Big Sodus Bay. A village of about thirty houses, which had been named Troupville, after an active politician of the day, but was more commonly known as Sodus, stood on the high ridge of land which almost surrounds that fine basin of water. The bar at the mouth of the harbor prevented the passage of any of his vessels, but the boats were sent in on the evening of the 19th and the storehouses were found to contain about 800 barrels of provisions. These were at once removed. Most of the inhabitants had deserted the place without offering any opposition. As the last boat was leaving the shore a party of men in plain clothes advanced and fired upon it, wounding several men. It was fast growing dark, but a landing was again effected and their assailants were quickly dispersed and driven into the woods. In this skirmish three privates of the Royal Scots were killed and a sergeant and four privates wounded. The attack upon the boats was actually made by a body of New York militia, consisting of detachments from Colonel Swift's regiment and Granger's battalion of riflemen, belonging to General Burnet's brigade, which had been assembled for the defence of the coast immediately after the descent at the mouth of the Genesee on the 15th. The greater part of the stores deposited at Sodus had been already removed into the interior by their assistance and they had marched homewards that very day. When the British squadron appeared they were hastily summoned to return, with the consequences already described. One militia man was killed and three wounded. By Sir James Yeo the attack was attributed entirely to the unfortunate inhabitants, whom he determined to punish and intimidate by the destruction of their village. Accordingly a party was again landed next morning, (Sunday, 20th June,) for this purpose. Long experience in similar operations on the coasts of France and Spain had made officers and men thoroughly proficient in such matters. The warehouses and six of the largest dwellings were destroyed, among the latter the handsome residence of the agent of Sir William Pulteney, who owned a large tract of land in the vicinity. The village tavern alone was spared because it was found to contain a wounded man, who was supposed to be dying. The squadron then sailed directly to Forty Mile Creek, where the captured supplies were landed, much to the relief of General Vincent, who had hitherto been prevented by the want of provisions and camp equipage combined from moving any considerable part of his division much in advance of that place, which he considered a very defensible position. Most of his force was actually suffering extreme distress from the want of such necessary articles as shirts, shoes and stockings. Captain Fulton informed the Governor General at this time that the 41st were "in rags and without shoes" and the 49th "literally naked." The arrival of the fleet relieved them at least from immediate danger of starvation, and they were strengthened at the same time by the arrival of two companies of the 104th and 340 Indians, comprising nearly all the warriors of the Seven Nations of Lower Canada. The latter force had been organized in May at Montreal by Sir John Johnson and consisted of 160 warriors from the Sault St. Louis, 120 from the Lake of Two Mountains and sixty from the St. Regis Village. They were officered by Captain Dominique Ducharne and Lieutenants J. B. DeLorimier, Gideon Gaucher, Louis Langlade, Evangeliste St. Germain, and Isaac LeClair, and embarked in canoes at Lachine on the 26th of that month. Lieut. St. Germain with the advance arrived at Kingston in time to take part in the expedition against Sackett's Harbor, and his promptitude in leading the attack on some American boats conveying troops to that place contributed largely to the success of the first day's operations on that occasion.

The cause of their subsequent detention is not stated, but they failed to join Vincent until the 20th of June, when they were at once sent forward to support Merritt and FitzGibbon. At the same time Colonel Bisshopp with a small brigade of light troops was thrown forward "to feel the pulse of the enemy." Bisshopp established his headquarters on the heights at the Twenty and detached Major P. V. DeHaren to occupy the bridge over the Twelve at St. Catharines with the two companies of the 104th and the light company of the 8th. The Indians were pushed on beyond the Ten, and a chain of outposts formed from the lake to Turney's cross roads, within a mile of the present town of Thorold. This position had a front of about seven miles, and every road by which a large body of troops could advance was occupied in considerable force.

During the day some of FitzGibbon's scouts had taken one of Chapin's men near Lundy's Lane, and learned that his whole troop had passed southward a few hours before. In the night Merritt, FitzGibbon and some other officers rode swiftly across the country to Point Abino to seize a spy. They succeeded in taking him and another of Chapin's troopers, and returned by daybreak. Fitz-Gibbon then advanced along Lundy's Lane in hope of intercepting Chapin on this return, but learned that he had been joined by Captain Myer, with 150 infantry from Fort George. Riding on alone to recomoitre he encountered two American soldiers, both of whom he succeeded in capturing with the assistance of some of the loyal inhabitants after a hard struggle, in which his agility and great strength were taxed to the utmost. Another of the enemy was killed by one of his men.

On the 23rd Captain Ducharme with twenty-five of his Indians passed quite around the enemy's position until he reached the bank of the river, within sight of Fort George. While there they discovered a barge filled with American soldiers on its way down from Lewiston, which they captured, killing four men and taking seven prisoners. They were hotly pursued by a party of dragoons but escaped by taking to the woods, with the exception of a single Iroquois warrior who rashly lagged behind in the hope of capturing a horse from the enemy.

General Dearborn felt that his situation was daily becoming less endurable. Ever since he had arrived on this frontier he had been in feeble health and scarcely fit for command. On the 8th of June, while yet smarting from the disaster of Stoney Creek, he had written the Secretary of War : "My ill state of health renders it extremely painful to attend to current duties, and unless it improves soon I fear I shall be compelled to retire to some place where my mind may be more at ease."

On the 20th he described his position in these despondent terms :

"From resignations, sickness and other causes, the number of regimental officers present and fit for duty is far below what the service requires. A considerable portion of the army being new recruits and the weather being unfavorable to health, the sick have become so numerous, in addition to the wounded, as to reduce the effective force far below what could have been contemplated. The enemy have been reinforced with about five hundred men of the 104th Regiment, whence I conclude he will endeavor to keep up such a plan at and near the head of the lake as will prevent any part of this army from joining or proceeding to Sackett's Harbor to attack Kingston, and such is the state of the roads in this flat country in consequence of continued rain as to render any operations against the enemy extremely difficult without the aid of a fleet for the transportation of provisions, ammunition and other necessary supplies. The enemy would probably retreat on our approach and keep out of our reach, being covered by one or more armed vessels. The whole of these embarrassments have resulted from a temporary loss of the command of the lake."

The audacity and success of the British scouting parties caused him so much annoyance that he consented to the wholesale deportation of the inhabitants, and applied to Erastus Granger, the Indian agent at Buffalo, for the assistance of 150 warriors of the Six Nations to be employed at the outposts.

Granger instantly sent a messenger to the chiefs of the villages at Alleghany requiring their services, but the Indians were ominously slow in obeying the summons, and two weeks elapsed before they actually appeared at Buffalo.

On returning from his latest foray Major Chapin warmly advocated an immediate attack on FitzGibbon's advanced post at DeCew's house, which he represented that he had closely examined, although it subsequently appeared that he had not been within four or five miles of that place, and did not even know the road to it after he had offered to act as guide to the expedition. FitzGibbon's force was described with more accuracy to consist of a single company of regular infantry and from sixty to one hundred Indians. The presence of a British outpost at St. Catharines had also been ascertained, but nothing was known of the presence of the Indians led by Ducharme encamped between these posts.

It was determined to make a simultaneous movement against both FitzGibbon and DeHaren, and on the afternoon of the 23d June the column designed to attack the former, having nearly twice the distance to travel, marched to Queenston. It consisted of nearly six hundred men, with two guns, under Lieut. Colonel Boerstler, who was considered a very efficient officer. For some reason, which is not stated, the movement against St. Catharines was then abandoned and DeHaren was permitted to carry his force to FitzGibbon's assistance, but not before the latter had succeeded in compelling Boerstler to surrender with his entire command, including Chapin's detested troop of marauders. General Dearborn's official letter states that only one man escaped, but Captain Merritt relates in his journal that six were believed to have got off, among whom was the notorious Totman.

General Dearborn was quite stunned by this amazing disaster. He had described the check at Stoney Creek as "a strange fatality," and he now referred to this affair as "an unfortunate and unaccountable event." In the panic in his camp which followed, many officers of rank urged that the army should at once retire across the river, but a council of war finally decided to maintain their position. The boats, which had been held in readiness for a movement of some kind, were moored under the guns of Fort Niagara, and an entrenched camp large enough to cover the entire force was formed on the right of Fort George.

These repeated checks caused unbounded disappointment at Washington, where Congress was then sitting, and there was an immediate outcry for Dearborn's removal from a command in which he had been so unsuccessful. "Dearborn's blunders," John Lovett, a Federalist, wrote from the capital on the 22d June, "especially in suffering the little army at Fort George to escape and preparing the way for the capture of Generals Chandler and Winder on the 6th of June, and leaving the way open for Procter's retreat and junction with the army at the head of the lake, create great heartburnings. It is probable Wilkinson will supersede Dearborn."

General Armstrong, the Secretary of War, frankly expressed his indignation. "Your letters of the 6th and 8th received," he wrote to the unhappy Dearborn on the 19th of June. "There is indeed some strange fatality attending our efforts. I cannot conceal from you the surprise occasioned by the two escapes of a beaten enemy, first on the 27th ult. and again on the 6th inst. Battles are not gained when an inferior and broken enemy is not destroyed. Should Procter have retired from Malden and effected a junction with Vincent, it has been done either to dispute possession of the peninsula or to effect their general retreat to Kingston. The latter, more probable." Harrison, he assured him, would effect a diversion in his favor with 3,500 regulars, by way of Detroit, while General Hampton would assemble a division of 4,000 more on Lake Champlain.

"If Yeo should defeat Chauncey," he added, "you should hold both Forts George and Erie. If otherwise, York is the best point to control the Canadian population and to prevent all intercourse between the enemy and the Indians."

The opponents of the administration exulted loudly over its failures. It was remarked that a year before General Chandler had proposed this toast at a public dinner: "The fourth of July, 1813 —May we drink wine on that day within the walls of Quebec," and that he would now have an opportunity of gratifying his wish as a prisoner of war. They made up the "Canadian Account Current" in these terms:

Debtor.	*Creditor.*
One territory.	One speaker's mace.
Seven generals.	One well cured scalp.
Two armies.	One log house.
Six millions per month.	One dead Indian more or less.

When information of the disaster at Beaver Dams arrived Mr. Ingersoll, a leader of the war party in Congress, relates that it was regarded as "the climax to continued tidings of mismanagement and misfortune. On the 6th of July, therefore, after a short accidental communion of regret and impatience in the lobby with the speaker, (Henry Clay), and General Ringgold of Maryland, I was deputed a volunteer to wait on the President and request General Dearborn's removal from a command which so far had proved so unfortunate."

A despatch from the Secretary of War was accordingly written the same day to General Dearborn, directing him to retire "until his health should be re-established," and instructing General Boyd, upon whom the command of the division devolved, "not to prosecute any offensive operation until our ascendency on the lake is re-established."

These orders did not reach Fort George until the 14th of July, but during the interval of twenty days which elapsed the American commander did not make the slightest attempt to resume the offensive.

The misfortunes of the invading army may be attributed partly, it is true, to the incompetence of the principal officers and the loss of the command of the lake, but still more to the astonishing lack of discipline and all soldierly attributes in the great mass of the men. Many had been enlisted during the winter in the seaboard towns and were almost immediately marched or transported rapidly about four hundred miles, in the months of March and April amid fierce storms of snow and rain, to the Canadian frontier. The last half of the journey was performed through a scantily inhabited country, where they had little opportunity to rest or cook their food. The hurried movement of two brigades from Lake Champlain to Sackett's Harbor was made in the face of a furious snowstorm, by which many soldiers were severely frost-bitten. During the voyage to York, they were crowded into vessels on which they had scarcely room to lie down, and were unavoidably exposed to the weather. After re-embarking, the fleet had been wind-bound in the harbor for four days, during which the men were constantly drenched with rain. Other detachments proceeding in open boats from Sackett's Harbor to Niagara suffered nearly as much discomfort. It is not surprising to learn that numbers on landing went directly into the hospital. The physique of the private soldiers was generally inferior. There was a total want of enthusiasm and *esprit de corps* among them.

General Dearborn seems to have been fully aware of these defects and made resolute efforts to remedy them. Fort George was strengthened by a deep ditch and line of palisades. The camp was surrounded by a ditch and earthworks, upon which about twenty pieces of cannon were mounted. When not employed on the fortifications the troops were diligently exercised. It was observed that for several days after Colonel Boerstler's defeat they did not venture to send even so much as a foraging or scouting party more than a mile beyond their lines.

The Canadian Indians at once retired to the Forty Mile Creek to celebrate their success by the usual festivities. They expected that the arms and stores taken at Beaver Dams would be divided among them and that they would receive head-money for the prisoners. They were therefore much discontented when they found that these expectations were not likely to be gratified, and threatened to return home. They complained that they had no shoes and could not go into the woods without them. A council was held to pacify them, and after receiving an assurance that their services would be suitably rewarded, and that the wounded and the families of any that might be killed would be taken care of, they consented to advance again.

Without waiting for their decision, Vincent moved forward his headquarters to St. Catharines and pushed on his outposts to the Four Mile Creek, with the intention of confining the enemy within their works as closely as possible.

Soon after his arrival at Kingston the Governor-General became convinced that Sir Roger Sheaffe had "absolutely lost the confidence of the inhabitants," and resolved to relieve him at once of the civil and military administration of the affairs of the Province. Major-General Francis De Rottenburg, then commanding the Montreal District, was selected to replace him. On the 29th of June General De Rottenburg arrived at Vincent's headquarters and assumed command. He was a Swiss by birth and had received his early military training in the Dutch army. In 1795 he entered the British service as major in Hompesch's Hussars. He served in the suppression of the rebellion in Ireland in 1798, and in the expeditions against Surinam and Walcheren and at the siege of Flushing. Sixty-four years of age, phlegmatic and unenterprising, his past career had not been distinguished and he was decidedly inferior to Vincent in vigor and capacity.

Almost his first official act was to direct the trial by court-marshal of two deserters taken in arms at Stoney Creek, who were found guilty and sentenced to death. Skirmishes at the outposts became a matter of daily and almost hourly occurrence. A letter from the American camp, dated on the last day of June, gives this gloomy picture of their situation:

"Our army, numbering about 2,000, is intrenched on the right of the fort. Fort Niagara is garrisoned by about 400 men. Our pickets and foraging parties are constantly harassed by loyal militia and Indians. Every night there is a skirmish. They keep our troops under arms, which exhausts and wears them away very fast. Our force has diminished very much. The enemy's fleet plagues our troops very much. It has been making demonstrations off Niagara for near two weeks. The weather is very wet. It rains at least one-half the time."

On the first of July the British outposts were extended to St. Davids, entirely cutting off all intercourse between the enemy's camp and the surrounding country and restricting their foragers to the narrow space between the lines. The road along the western bank of the Four Mile Creek afforded a very good and easy means of communicating between these outposts, a decided advantage over the American piquets, which were separated from each other by enclosures and woods. Of the latter there were six, usually numbered from the right, covering the front of their position from lake to river about a mile in advance of their intrenchments and nearly half a mile apart.

Yeo's squadron continued to blockade the mouth of the river for a week after its return, occasionally cruising eastward along the American shore of the lake to intercept any small craft that might attempt to steal along the coast from the Genesee. During this time four small vessels and several Durham boats loaded with provisions for the American army were taken on their way to Fort Niagara. A captured sailor, one William Howells, was induced to act as a pilot, and the boats of the squadron under his guidance searched every bay and creek where a boat could lie hidden as far as the mouth of the Genesee, and much alarm was excited in the American commissariat lest they should ascend the river and destroy a magazine and the bridge on the main highway for supplies from the east, known as the Ridge Road, by which all communication with their base of supplies would be effectively interrupted for some time. On the 29th, however, Yeo was forced to return to Kingston for provisions.

But, on the other hand, a small schooner, the *Lady Murray*, bringing from Kingston a much needed supply of ammunition and a "choice collection of every kind of stores," was taken by the American despatch boat, the *Lady of the Lake*. At the time, this was felt to be an almost irreparable loss, and strict orders were given to limit the wasteful expenditure of powder by the Indians. They were informed that "pigeon shooting and such idle sport must be given up." Colonel Claus, their superintendent, complained bitterly that the Indians of the Grand River did not set a good example to those that had come from a distance. Only about half of them had joined the army. The others roamed lawlessly about the country committing outrages. "They plunder the settlers and return home to deposit what they take from the inhabitants. They destroy every hog and sheep they can meet with."

The effectiveness of the blockade of his position on three sides was such that General Dearborn was then forced to draw his supplies from Buffalo, by the road leading along the American side of the river from Schlosser at the upper end of the portage around the falls, where they were landed from boats plying above. Ensign Winder of FitzGibbon's company took possession of Chippawa with a small detachment, and soon ascertained that the American block-house nearly opposite was weakly guarded and might be easily surprised. On the afternoon of the 4th July, FitzGibbon invited Lieut.-Colonel Thomas Clark of the 2d Lincoln Militia to co-operate with Winder in an attempt upon it that night, when it was anticipated that the guard would be more than usually negligent from the effects of the festivities of the day. Clark assembled thirty-four officers and men of his regiment, and being joined by Winder with Volunteer Thompson and six privates of the 49th, em-barked in three boats. They landed at daybreak, and took the block-house with its entire guard, consisting of two officers, nine privates,. three civilians, and three Canadian refugees, without the least resis-tance. A small gunboat, two bateaux, a brass six-pounder, fifty-seven stand of arms and a considerable quantity of ammunition and pro-visions were brought away. Sixteen tons of cannon-shot were thrown into the river, and six scows and the same number of large boats were partially destroyed. The removal and destruction of these stores occupied about an hour, during which they were not molested, but after entering their boats to re-cross the river a party of a dozen men, supposed to be workmen from Porter's Mills at the Falls, appeared on the bank and commenced an ineffective fire upon them.

This successful descent excited quite a disproportionate alarm all along the American side of the river and caused the inhabitants of Black Rock and Buffalo to clamor for military protection. At the former place General Peter B. Porter had already assembled a volunteer force with the intention of crossing the river and forming an intrenched camp nearly opposite, where a site had been selected. He had even proposed to march down the Canadian side and attack the British post at St. Davids. These projects were now abandoned, and he began preparations for the defence of his own position. A party which he had sent over on the morning of the 5th to remove the family of a refugee, hastily retired on the approach of a detach-ment of Canadian militia which took post near the ferry landing, and a brisk cannonade was opened across the river by the American batteries.

On the same day, 150 Western Indians, conducted by Captain Matthew Elliott and Blackbird, the Ottawa chief who had commanded at the slaughter of the Chicago garrison the year before, arrived at De Rottenburg's headquarters. These were chiefly Ottawas and Chippewas from the wilds north of Lake Huron, and Procter wrote that there were "some very fine fellows" among them whom he might miss. De Rottenburg, probably with equal truth, described them as "a most ferocious and savage set." They were at once sent forward to join the remainder in their encampment near the Four Mile Creek, where they were joyfully welcomed.

Some days previous to their arrival several of the American Tuscaroras had appeared on the opposite bank of the river near Lewiston and signified their wish to speak with the principal chiefs of the Six Nations living in Canada. Accordingly, that same afternoon, the chiefs of the sixteen nations then represented in the Indian camp, accompanied by Interpreters Brant and Fairchild, went to the appointed place on the river, when a party of ten Tuscaroras approached on the other side and they shouted to each other across the roaring torrent. The Tuscaroras began the conversation by affirming their friendship and inquiring whether the others were still friends to them. Katvirota, speaker of the Onondagas, eldest of the Six Nations, replied haughtily that although it had been said that the British were weak, yet "the Great Spirit is with us and we are enabled to take possession again. As the King has been obliged to give ground at Niagara, we want to understand from you whether you are induced to take part with the Americans or not." The Tuscaroras rejoined, "These times have been very hard, under difficulties, being so near the lines, and we wish to know whether your sentiments are still friendly toward us, and if you cross the river whether you will hurt us." Katvirota retorted in the same arrogant tone as before: "This will depend on yourselves. If you take no part with the Americans we shall meet you with the same friendship we ever did, and we look for the day when you will see our faces on your side of the water. We have no contention with you: it is King and the Americans, and we have taken part with the King. We will contend for his right." The Tuscarora stated in reply that they had determined to "sit quiet and take no part," but that a great council would be held at Buffalo in five days, and the conference then ended.

After the evacuation of Fort George a quantity of medicines and hospital stores had been buried near the house of a faithful old loyalist at the Two Mile Creek, Castell Chorus, once a soldier in a German regiment in Burgoyne's army, and after his escape from captivity, in Butler's Rangers. This house stood close to one of the American outposts, but the necessities of the division had made it highly important to recover the stores even at the risk of provoking an engagement. Accordingly, the light company of the King's Regiment under Lieut. Collis was detailed for the purpose, with Captain Merritt as guide, and late on the evening of the 7th Colonel Claus was instructed to assemble a body of Indians to act as a covering party for the waggons. The Indians were directed to occupy a position in front of Chorus's house by two o'clock in the morning, but failed to leave their camp until broad daylight, when about a hundred went forward under Norton and Blackbird and the Interpreters Brisbois, Langlade and Lyons. The stores were recovered without molestation, and the soldiers retired with the waggons, while the two officers remained to breakfast at Peter Ball's house. The Indians loitered behind and began a brisk skirmish with the enemy's picket, which they finally drove from its post. They continued in this way to annoy the American outposts until the middle of the afternoon, when several hundred infantry came out from their intrenchments and they instantly retired with the hope of drawing the whole party forward into the wood and ravines near the Cross Roads, where the remainder of their warriors lay concealed. These well-worn tactics were partially successful. Lieut. Eldridge, Adjutant of the 13th United States Infantry, who had already distinguished himself on the retreat from Stoney Creek, being far in advance, rushed blindly in pursuit at the head of about forty men. A single volley from the ambush struck down eighteen of his followers. The remainder instantly turned and ran back, while the Indians rushed forward from their coverts to cut off their retreat. Eldridge wounded one of his pursuers with a pistol shot and was promptly shot down and tomahawked by another. Twelve were taken prisoners, and of the whole party only five escaped. Besides the three officers of the Indian department and Captain Merritt and John Ball, both of whom were unarmed, the only white person present on this occasion was John Lawe, a boy of thirteen years, who lived close by. His father, Captain George Lawe of the 1st Lincoln Militia, had been badly wounded and an elder brother killed in the battle of Fort George. After being allowed to return home on parole, his father had been arrested and carried off as a prisoner. Animated by a fierce passion for revenge, this boy seized a musket when the firing began and joined the Indians. He continued to load and fire in the most fearless manner until the skirmish had nearly ended, when his mother appeared and forcibly removed him. Of the prisoners, three were surrendered to Colonel Claus that night, the remainder were maliciously retained by the Indians until next morning for the purpose of thoroughly frightening them. Although these barbarous practices had been strictly prohibited by the officers in charge of them, the wild Western Indians not only scalped but savagely mutilated the bodies of the dead before leaving the field. When tasked with this misconduct, Blackbird alleged that the Americans had mangled the dead Indians at the Miami Rapids a few months before. "They were not satisfied with having killed them," he said, "but cut them into small pieces. This made us very angry. My words to my people were as long as the powder burnt to kill and scalp. * * * * If the Big Knives after they kill people of our color leave them without hacking them to pieces, we will follow their example. They have themselves to blame. The way they treat our killed and the remains of those that are in their graves to the west makes our people mad when they meet the Big Knives. Whenever they can get any of our people into their hands they cut them like meat into small pieces." Only the Interpreter Langlade and two of the Indians were wounded in this affair, in which Claus estimated, probably with considerable exaggeration, that the Americans had lost upwards of one hundred men.

While this skirmish was in progress at Butler's farm, the Seven Nations of Lower Canada were holding a council at the Ten Mile Creek, at which they told Claus that they intended to return home. "Our patience is at an end," they said. "The King has enemies below as well as here. This is the day our people begin to cut grass for their cattle and we must prepare not to let our people and cattle starve. * * * We took a good many things the other day (at Beaver Dams.) What are we to get?"

Claus assured them that their families would receive assistance in harvesting, and that they would be paid for the "things" they had taken, and after some deliberation they seemed perfectly satisfied and agreed to remain for some time longer.

The discovery of the mangled bodies at the scene of Eldridge's disaster thrilled the American camp with horror and indignation, and occasioned a renewed demand for the employment of Indians on their own behalf. The inhabitants of the vicinity were accused not without reason of hostility and ordered to leave their homes under penalty of the severest punishment.

One of De Rottenburg's first measures was to secure Burlington against a sudden attack by throwing up intrenchments and mounting cannon, as he regarded that position as a stronghold to which he might eventually be forced to retire in the hope of maintaining it until Yeo would be able to co-operate in an attack on the forts at the mouth of the Niagara. The latter had just been thwarted in the execution of a bold and well-planned attempt to destroy the American fleet at its anchorage in Sackett's Harbor, which, if successful, would have given him absolute control of the lake. Embarking 400 picked seamen and 250 soldiers in row boats the very next day after his return to Kingston, he crossed the lake and landed his men on the uninhabited shore of Point Peninsula in full view and only about ten miles from the harbor, where boats and men remained concealed in the dense woods for twenty-four hours, intending to make the attack on the following night. But two men of the Newfoundland Regiment deserted from the garrison at Kingston immediately after Yeo's departure, and, dogging his boats until they landed, made their way to the American lines with this important intelligence. The hurry and bustle with which the ships were manned and put in a posture of defence next day convinced Yeo, who was intently observing them with a glass from his hiding place, that the alarm had been given, and he returned empty-handed to Kingston on the morning of the 2d July. The fine new ship *General Pike*, for which Chauncey had been waiting in port for the last month, was seen to be nearly ready for sea. She was known to carry 28 heavy guns, with a crew of 400 men, and believed to be almost a match for the entire British squadron. Yeo was obliged to content himself with watching the harbor's mouth and cutting off supplies. A few days later his gunboats destroyed the barracks at Gravelly Point and brought off a boat with 100 barrels of provisions and a large quantity of oars.

On learning of Yeo's failure, De Rottenburg good-humoredly remarked, "*A mauvais jeu, il faut faire bonne mine*," and made vigorous efforts to repair the roads in his rear, which he described as the worst he ever saw, to facilitate a retreat when it became unavoidable. He complained that with the exception of Harvey, whom he characterized as "most active, zealous, and intelligent," the heads of the departments were "deficient in activity and cleverness," and that the militia staff in particular was "miserable."

On the 6th of July he detached 120 men of the 41st to assist Procter, who was bitterly complaining that the reinforcement had been so long withheld, and promised to send him one hundred more as soon as the remainder of 104th and the 1st battalion of the Royal Scots arrived.

In the hope of making a slight diversion in Procter's favor and destroying the naval stores at Black Rock, he authorized Lieutenant-Colonel Bisshopp, on the 9th, to attempt the surprise of that place. A couple of nights before this, some of Bisshopp's scouts had crossed the river near the head of Grand Island, captured some provision waggons and ascertained that Black Rock was then only garrisoned by militia. On the 10th, however, Colonel Brady arrived from Erie with 300 regulars, and by direction of General Dearborn, left half of them to assist Porter in its defence. Five hundred militia had been called out ten days before, but not more than half that number had mustered. In addition to these, the inhabitants had been embodied and armed for service. About one hundred Indians had assembled in response to Granger's appeal. But this force, though respectable in point of numbers, was too widely scattered to be very formidable even for defence. One hundred of the regulars and a party of militia were stationed at Buffalo. Another detachment of 150 militia occupied a battery called Fort Gibson, half a mile above the village of Black Rock, which was armed with three guns. The remainder were distributed in the village, the main body being quartered in a log blockhouse surrounded by earthworks, also mounting three guns, with strong outposts in the Marine Barracks at the navy yard, and a redoubt commanding the bridge over Shogeoquady Creek, on the road to Tonawanda, each being defended by an additional gun.

The force selected for the attack by Bisshopp was small but efficient, consisting of twenty men of the Royal Artillery under Lieutenant (afterwards Major-General) R. S. Armstrong, forty of the 8th, Lieutenant Barstow; 100 of the 41st, Captain Saunders; forty of the 49th, Lieut. FitzGibbon, and forty of the 2d and 3d Lincoln Militia, Lieutenant-Colonel Thomas Clark. Bisshopp determined to command in person, and it was intended that the detachment of the 41st should proceed to join General Procter immediately after.

The expedition left Chippawa about two o'clock in the morning of the 11th and landed three miles below Black Rock half an hour before daylight. The militia guard in the redoubt at the bridgehead abandoned their post in such haste and confusion that they did not even give the alarm to the party in the Marine Barracks near by, most of whom were surprised and taken by FitzGibbon, who led the advance with the 49th. Bisshopp pressed swiftly forward, took possession of Fort Tompkins almost without resistance, and advanced within two hundred yards of Fort Gibson before his approach was discovered. General Porter had been on the alert nearly all night in expectation of an attack, but had gone to bed in his own house and fallen asleep shortly before daybreak. When he awoke the British were in full possession of the batteries, and he barely effected his escape through the window, passing between their advance and main body, and made his way to Buffalo by a circuitous route, on foot and alone. The militia in Fort Gibson abandoned their artillery and stores and retreated in the same direction, following the beach. On the way they met the regulars moving to their support, and the whole body then retired together. Bisshopp remained in undisturbed possession of Black Rock for two hours, which he occupied in burning the block-houses, barracks and navy yard, with a large schooner moored there, in dismantling the batteries and destroying the stores that he had no means of removing, and in loading the remainder on a captured scow and seven large bateaux. So far his success had been cheap and complete.

Perceiving that there was no pursuit, General Porter rallied his scattered forces, and being joined by the regulars, Buffalo militia, and Indians, with a field-gun, advanced by a round-about course through the fields and roads until he gained the skirts of the village. Then, as the British were embarking in some confusion, he briskly attacked their rear. Bisshopp re-landed without an instant's hesitation and drove the assailants into the woods. But in retiring to the boats again, Captain Saunders of the 41st fell mortally wounded and several men of the same regiment were disabled and left behind. Then one of the boats grounded on the bar as it was leaving the harbor in such a position that it was exposed for several minutes to the fire of nearly three hundred men. Two others gallantly returned to the rescue, assisted the crew of the stranded boat to get afloat and towed it off. But this was not accomplished without severe loss. In all thirteen were killed, twenty-seven wounded and six reported missing. Bisshopp and Clark, who were conspicuous alike by their uniform and exertions, were both hit. Clark's injury was slight, but Bisshopp was badly wounded in both arms and the thigh. Although not at first supposed to be dangerous, these wounds proved mortal, and that distinguished officer died on the fifth day after.* Of the detachment of the 41st, Capt. Saunders and six men were killed, Ensign Mompesson, a sergeant and ten men were wounded, and four privates missing. Having thus lost nearly a fourth of its numbers, it was prevented from continuing its march to Detroit. Exclusive of fifteen or twenty prisoners taken in the batteries, who were chiefly sailors and regular artillery men detailed to serve the guns, General Porter reported vaguely that he had lost two or three men killed and eight or ten wounded—two of the latter being Indians.

The aims of the expedition had been fully accomplished before the retreat was begun, and had Bisshopp adhered strictly to the letter of his instructions he might have come off without the loss of a man. Four field guns and great quantities of provisions and naval and military stores were brought away in a captured scow and seven large boats, which were loaded to the water's edge. Four heavier guns with their carriages were destroyed, and the remainder of the stores thrown into the river. The acquisition of these supplies was a distinct relief to De Rottenburg, and their loss on

---

* Lieut.-Colonel Bisshopp was barely thirty at the time of his death. He lies buried in the grave-yard on Lundy Lane's battlefield. In Parham village church in Sussex, near the stately Elizabethan mansion where he was born, there is a memorial tablet with these lines:

"His pillow—knot of sturdy oak !
His shroud—a so'dier's simple cloak !
His dirge—will sound till Time's no more—
Niagara's loud and solemn roar.
There Cecil lies—say where the grave
More worthy of a Briton brave !"

the other hand greatly delayed the equipment of the American squadron on Lake Erie.

These events also strongly tended to aggravate the depression of the American cabinet, which had so confidently undertaken to direct the campaign from Washington.

John Lovett, a Federalist member of Congress, wrote to a friend on the 17th of July, immediately after the news had been received there:

"The British back of Fort George have lately driven in the picket guard, killed some and took forty or fifty attempting to reinforce the guard. They have also crossed to Black Rock and destroyed stores there. The Postmaster-General this morning, relating these things, exclaimed, 'It does seem as if the very Devil is in our luck.'"

The effect upon the blockaded army was of course not less discouraging. "The enemy," De Rottenburg wrote, "is in much fear of being attacked and harass their men by continual nightly duties."

Although General Dearborn absolutely refrained from any forward movement and had declined to sanction the attempt proposed by General Porter upon St. Davids on the ground that the British force above that place would render the enterprise "more hazardous than present circumstances will permit," his patrols and pickets were constantly attacked almost in sight of his lines. On the 11th, a party of Algonquin and Nippissing Indians, led by the interpreter Langlade, waylaid eight American dragoons near Ball's house—killed two and captured the quartermaster's sergeant, a Frenchman. Late in the afternoon of the same day, ten of the St. Joseph's band had a prolonged skirmish with a much superior number of infantry, in which they lost one warrior mortally wounded.

Three days later General Dearborn retired from command of the American army and was succeeded by Brigadier-General John P. Boyd, as Major-General Lewis had been recently removed to Sackett's Harbor, where a division of troops was being assembled for the protection of the fleet. Boyd had entered the United States army as a subaltern at an early age, but soon resigned his commission and went to India where he remained for many years and rose to high rank in the service of the Nizam of Hyderabad. When the attack upon the Chesapeake seemed likely to cause a war, General Armstrong, the present Secretary of War, then American Minister in France, found him in Paris and had him appointed a colonel of infantry in the re-organized army. He had commanded the regulars in the battle of Tippecanoe and was nominated as a brigadier-general in recognition of his services on that occasion.

He was now "forbidden to engage in any affair with the enemy that could be avoided," and subjected to the orders of Major-Generals Hampton and Lewis, one of whom was at Burlington, Vt., and the other at Sackett's Harbor. One of the Secretary's latest letters to his predecessor, written, too, before the recent disasters were known, had strictly enjoined caution. "The leisure you now have," he said, "affords a fine opportunity for the adjutants and inspectors-general to attend to their particular duties. Some of the parties of which you speak from the enemy may practice a trick on those who follow them. *These last ought to be very circumspect.*" The fate of Boerstler and Eldridge had since given emphasis to the warning. Boyd was only regarded as a stop-gap until a leader of more reputation could be secured. Armstrong had already offered the post to Major-General James Wilkinson, with whom he had served on the staff of General Gates in the revolution. "Why should you remain in your land of *cypress*," he wrote, "when patriotism and ambition invite you to one where grows the *laurel?*......If our cards be well played we may renew the scenes of Saratoga." The latter, however, displayed an apparent if not a real reluctance to accept. Lovett wrote that "Wilkinson is making up his mind to take command of the northern army, considers the responsibility infinite, that he must conquer or die: lose all his fame or acquire more: that he will not undertake it unless he can be assured of the means to be put into his hands." Accordingly, more than a month elapsed before his objections could be overcome and he actually set out for the seat of war.

Even if he had not been restrained by his instructions, there was now little inclination in Boyd's command to attempt any offensive movement. Officers and men alike were profoundly depressed if not absolutely panic-stricken by an unbroken series of petty checks and reverses. Letters written from the camp complain bitterly of the constant annoyance to which they were exposed, but confess their inability to resent it. One of these written as early as the 29th of June says: "I am informed our army daily expects the arrival of 400 or 500 Tuscaroras and Senecas. The general intends, I understand, to accept of them, which I think would be important against the enemy now, for they are continually harassing our piquet and guards and detachments sent out into the country by parties composed of loyal militia and Indians and a few British regulars. Every night our troops have a skirmish with the marauders. They are very troublesome. They keep our troops under arms which exhausts them very much......Our men are in a wretched condition for clothing, many barefooted and half-naked. The supplies of the army from the quartermaster-general's department are irregular......The weather is very wet. It rains at least

one-half the time. The atmosphere is very changeable from very
warm to very cool days and nights. This produces sickness in the
troops." Another, on the 11th July, after relating the destruction of
Eldridge's command, states that "the enemy has advanced within a
few miles of us. The Indians are continually attacking our picket
guard. They are far too strong for us to attack them in the woods."
A third, dated the 16th, relates that "the enemy are reinforcing
every day. We are encircled, they are in our front, the lake in our
rear and flanks, and we do not hold any more ground than that on
which we stand." Still another, on the 17th, observes, "I think our
situation very critical. The enemy are nearly in sight of our pickets.
Their force is gaining every day : ours diminishing. We are attacked
and harassed every night......I have not had my clothes off for
two months." On the same day, General Porter informed the
Governor of New York that "the army are panic-stricken and the
affairs of this frontier most critical."

In fact, the arrival of several companies of the Royal Scots,
104th, had enabled General De Rottenburg to move his headquarters
to St. Davids and advance his outposts still closer to the American
camp. This, he said, "reduces the enemy to the ground he stands
upon, and prevents his getting any supplies from our territory.
Independently of these advantages, the more forward movement
became necessary on account of the Indian warriors. They must
be actively employed, and are now daily engaged with the enemy's
outposts, harassing and teasing them the whole day long......It is
surprising that with such a superiority of numbers he does not
attempt to drive me from my position, but keeps perfectly quiet
and passive within his lines."

The left of the new position rested on Servos's Mills, near the
mouth of the Four Mile Creek, where there was a secure shelter for
their supply boats, with piquets nearly a mile in advance on the Lake
Road. The centre occupied the Swamp Road at the crossing of the
creek, with piquets at Ball's farm. The bridges over the creek on
both these roads were protected by field-works. The artillery was
posted on the left and supported by the 104th. The battalion of
the King's, or 8th regiment, and a detachment of the 100th, with
the entire body of Indians, formed the centre, while the Royal Scots
and Glengarry Light Infantry held the ground in front of St. Davids
and Queenston, with their piquets thrown well forward. A strong
post of observation was established on Queenston Heights. The
outposts of the enemy were stationed at or near the houses of
Crooks, Secord, John Butler, Thomas Butler, McLellan, and Fields,
beyond the Two Mile Creek. Boyd's division was known to consist
of a battalion of light artillery, detachments of the 2d and 3d

United States artillery, the 2d dragoons, the 5th, 6th, 8th, 12th, 13th, 16th, 21st, 22d, 23d and 29th United States Infantry, and a battalion of volunteer riflemen, estimated at upwards of 5000 effective men.

A brisk encounter occurred while this movement was being made, of which there is this vivid narrative in the Ridout correspondence:

"On Saturday, 17th," says Mr. T. G. Ridout, "Henry Nelles and I rode down to the Cross Roads, three miles from Niagara, where the Royals, King's and 600 or 700 Indians are posted. I understood the Americans were advancing into Ball's fields. Immediately the yell was given and Blackbird and Norton set out with their followers to meet them. Nelles and I rode along, and in a few minutes the skirmish begun by the Western Indians getting upon the left flank and the Five Nations upon the other. The enemy consisted of 500 men. They soon retired, firing heavy volleys upon Blackbird's party, which was the nearest. The road is so straight I could see into town, and Nelles and I rode on with the Indians to within one and-a-quarter miles of Niagara, when we perceived a large reinforcement from them, with a piece of artillery, and they advanced with a large front, firing grape shot. The Indians scattered in the woods, but we were obliged to keep the road. By this time three companies of the Royals and a brass six-pounder came up and were posted on this side of Ball's field—the Yankees on the other side. We fired for some time, when the Americans thought fit to retreat. At one time, from the farther end of Ball's field a mile and a half this way the road was covered with Indians, officers, soldiers, and horses, and from the Presbyterian church they must have judged our force at 3000 men. We had about 1000. A good many Yankees were killed. One Indian took two scalps. A young Cayuga had his arm and side carried away with a cannon ball, and another had a ball through his arm."*

The force engaged on the part of the Americans consisted of a battalion of volunteers (the Irish Greens), a company of mounted infantry, four companies of riflemen, and four troops of dragoons, or about 1100 men, under Colonel Winfield Scott, and they admitted the loss of four killed and nine wounded, among the latter Major Armstrong, son of the Secretary of War, and Captain Towson.

The movement of troops and seamen from Fort Niagara towards Buffalo, although only designed for the defence of that place and manning the Lake Erie squadron, forced De Rottenburg to detach a strong party to Chippawa to protect the rear of his position, and

* Mrs. Edgar, Ten Years of Upper Canada, p. 204.

this in turn renewed the alarm on the opposite shore and occasioned the prolonged detention of the Indians assembled at Black Rock, much to the disappointment of General Boyd, who declared that their presence with his army would be "incalculably important," and that they were "certainly the most efficient troops for such a wood country as this."

Finally, in compliance with his insistent demands, General Porter and Mr. Granger invited these Indians, numbering between three or four hundred men, to proceed to Fort George, "not to invade the enemy's country, but to act as a piquet guard for his army." After the usual period of deliberation on this proposal, Porter reported that their spokesman, the celebrated Red Jacket, stated that they "had unanimously agreed to reject it for reasons assigned by them at large (and intermixed with no small share of sarcasm) which could not be but satisfactory, and which would do no credit to the army of the centre to repeat." He declared that they were ready to remain there with the volunteer militia and "to penetrate the enemy's country with them."

Porter then seized this opportunity of reviving his proposition to lead a force from Black Rock against the rear of the blockading army, to consist of about 1200 men, regulars, militia and Indians in equal numbers, with three or four field guns, to land at Chippawa at daybreak, "dispose of the British forces stationed there, and proceed immediately to St. Davids to join and co-operate with such part of your army as you might think prudent to send out." With such a body he confidently assured the Secretary of War, "I pledge myself to enter Canada and relieve his army from their distress."

"The truth is (and it is known to every man of common sense in this part of the country)," he continued, "that we have had an army at Fort George for two months past, which at any moment of this period might by a vigorous and well-directed expedition of three or four days have prostrated the whole of the enemy's force in this division of the country, and yet this army lies panic-stricken, shut up, and whipped in by a few hundred miserable savages, leaving the whole of this frontier, except the mile in extent which they occupy, exposed to the inroads and depredations of the enemy."

Major Chapin, who had escaped from captivity with most of his troop by overpowering a militia guard when on his way to Kingston, crossed the river with sixty volunteers to reconnoitre on the 21st July, and advanced as far as Frenchman's Creek without opposition.

Boyd's instructions, however, left him no discretion until the arrival of Chauncey's fleet should set him free to act.

Both parties felt that ultimate success was dependent on the mastery of the lake. In the absence of Yeo's squadron, now prolonged far beyond expectation, De Rottenburg's embarrassments hourly increased. Supplies dwindled away. Desertions, hitherto almost unknown, became alarmingly frequent as his outposts approached the enemy's works. Not less than fifteen men deserted within a few days from the 104th, ten alone from the two flank companies. Five grenadiers were taken in the attempt. In consequence of these disgraceful defections, the Royal Scots were ordered to relieve a regiment which until then had been distinguished for gallantry and good conduct. On the 9th July, James Grady, late a a private in the King's regiment but taken in arms at Stoney Creek, was shot, and ten days later two men of the 104th and one of the Royal Scots suffered the same fate for "example's sake." The Indians were then thrown forward into the woods beyond the outposts with instructions to shoot at sight any men attempting to pass over to the enemy, and desertions ceased at once. But these unstable auxiliaries soon again began to show signs of discontent. Blackbird was annoyed because Colonel Young had insisted that he should surrender the prisoners he had taken on the 8th of July, although a ransom was subsequently paid him. At any time it was scarcely possible to prevail upon them to act at night, the best time for beating up the enemy's outposts, as it was contrary to their usual custom. The prolonged absence of the squadron dismayed and alarmed them, and already the Western Indians began to talk of returning homewards and to wrangle over the distribution of the annual allowance of presents, which had not yet arrived. Colonel Claus held a council with them at the Cross Roads on the 21st July in the hope of appeasing their dissatisfaction, at which he assured them that the squadron was expected to sail from Kingston the day before, and that an attack upon the enemy's position would be made as soon as it arrived. These Indians then agreed to remain a few days longer. Four days later the Seven Nations of Lower Canada announced that they would only remain for ten days. At the latter meeting Claus remonstrated against the constant plundering of the wretched inhabitants.

"The General," he said, "wishes me to speak to you on behalf of the poor people about us, who have complained that they lose everything about their places, and he requests that you will exert yourselves to prevent these acts of cruelty. It is very hard upon these poor people, for on the one hand they are injured by the enemy, and on the other by us."

To this, a chief known as "The Echo" replied, "we are wrong, and confess our faults. It seemed as if these men wished to side with the strongest. We have taken many things, but any that are pointed out we will give up."

Norton and Claus had quarreled beyond hope of reconciliation, and as the Mohawk Chief bore the reputation of a brave and skilful leader and was, besides, a persuasive and forcible speaker, the influence of the latter gradually declined both with the General and the Indians.

About the end of July Norton was married by Mr. Addison to a girl belonging to the Delaware tribe, whom Claus spitefully described as the "daughter of a deserter from the Queen's Rangers and a common woman." and asserted that thenceforward, "he did nothing but ride about the country with madam and a posse of his connections."

In consequence of the persistent demands of the Indians for compensation for wounds and the death of relatives, a board of inquiry had been assembled at headquarters, which recommended that "with a view to soften and restrain the Indian warriors in their conduct to such Americans as may be made by them prisoners," they should receive :

"For every prisoner brought in alive, $5, to be paid immediately by the commissary on the certificate of the general officer commanding the division.

"To a chief for the loss of an eye or limb, $100 per annum, payable in money or goods.

"To a warrior for the loss of an eye or limb, or a wound held equivalent to the loss of an eye or limb, $70 per annum, payable in money or goods.

"To the widow of a chief killed in action, a present of $200.

"To the widow of a warrior killed in action, a present of $170."

On the 20th July, the first squadron of the 19th Light Dragoons arrived and relieved Captain Merritt's troop, which from constant and arduous service had become almost unfit for duty. "I found the horses battered and worn out," said Captain Hall, the inspector of cavalry, "with scarcely a shoe to their feet, many lamed for want of shoeing, and some of the horses unfit for light dragoon service in point of size, &c., and with the exception of a few and half-equipped saddles and a few swords and pistols, the men and horses are totally destitute of appointments."

Captain Coleman's troop of provincial cavalry, lately enlisted in Montreal, arrived about the same time, but half of it was at once sent forward to the Detroit.

The numerical superiority of the blockaded army alone was sufficient to render any serious movement upon its defences extremely hazardous, and the American fleet now seemed to be in a fair way to regain control of the lake, by which the very existence of De Rottenburg's division would be imperilled. As the Governor-General justly remarked, it was "not expedient to carry on decisive operations against Fort Niagara while the enemy are in a preponderating force on Lake Ontario, because, in my estimation, the first object to be attained is ascendency on the lake.

But Commodore Chauncey was straining every resource at his command with the same object, and he possessed an inestimable advantage in being much nearer his base of supplies and having an abundance of workmen. Guns, shot, cordage, iron-work, in fact everything required for the equipment of the British squadron, had to be brought from England.

The ship *General Pike* was launched by Chauncey on the 12th of June, and rapidly pushed to completion. She measured 140 feet in length by 37 feet beam, 900 tons, and mounted thirty-four 24-pounders, fourteen on a side on a flush deck, four on the top-gallant forecastle, one on a traversing carriage on the forecastle, and another mounted in the same way on the poop, giving her an effective broadside of eighteen guns. Her crew was said to number 420. The *Madison* was re-armed with twenty-two 32-pounders and manned with 340 men. A fast-sailing brig to carry twenty guns, the *Sylph*, was laid down as soon as the Pike was launched. After the failure of Yeo's attempt to surprise the place, a division of 3000 men, principally regular troops, was hurriedly assembled for the defence of Sackett's Harbor, where they remained idle all summer. A large floating battery for the protection of the harbor was built at Oswego, but went to pieces in a storm while on its way thither. Two detachments of veteran seamen, numbering 130, arrived from Boston about the end of June, followed on the 8th of July by the entire crew of the frigate *John Adams*. While thus engaged, Chauncey made no appearance upon the lake except by detaching three of his swiftest schooners to Niagara with seamen for the Lake Erie squadron, about the middle of July, but on the 23d he put out with two ships, a brig, and eleven schooners, having a tonnage of 2721, carrying 114 guns, throwing a broadside of 1629 pounds of shot, and manned by 1193 men. Nearly a quarter of these guns were mounted on pivot or traversing carriages and could fire in any direction, and were consequently as effective as twice the number mounted in broadside.

Meanwhile Yeo had been unable to augment the force of his squadron in any way except by a slight increase in its armament, and had actually been obliged to weaken the crews by detailing men for the inestimably important duty of patroling the St. Lawrence and keeping open the communication with Montreal.

With this object a squadron of nine small gunboats was equipped, each carrying two guns and from 27 to 40 men, organized in three divisions, one stationed at Kingston, one at Prescott and one at Gananoqui, to cruise among the Thousand Islands. Eight days elapsed after Chauncey's departure from Sackett's Harbor before the British commodore was able to sail in pursuit with six vessels of 1385 tons, mounting 92 guns throwing a broadside of 1374 pounds, and manned by 632 men exclusive of 200 soldiers of the Royal Newfoundland and 100th regiments as marines. The armament of his squadron was most formidable in close action, and Yeo declared his intention to seek this at all hazards. Prevost described the squadron as being "powerfully armed, well equipped, completely manned and ably commanded," and added, "it is scarcely possible a decisive action can be avoided, and I therefore humbly hope H. R. H. the Prince Regent will approve of its being courted by us as a necessary measure for the preservation of the advanced positions of this army, which I have determined to maintain until the naval ascendency on Lake Ontario is decided, convinced that a retrograde movement would eventually endanger the safety of a large proportion of the troops in Upper Canada and convert the heart of the province into the seat of war."

Before sailing, General Boyd had informed Chauncey that from information received from Major Chapin and other escaped prisoners as well as deserters, he had ascertained that a valuable magazine of supplies and captured ordnance had been formed at Burlington, which was reported to be guarded only by about 150 men, and suggested that this post might be surprised by a small land force embarked from Niagara on his fleet. On the 26th July the *Lady of the Lake* arrived with a message from the latter that he entirely approved, and that he would proceed at once to Burlington with his whole fleet, but needed information and guides. Colonel Winfield Scott with a company of artillery, accompanied by Major Chapin and several refugees and deserters as guides, embarked on this vessel, which rejoined the fleet on the evening of the same day. On consultation, it was then decided to put into Niagara and take on board 250 infantry, which was accomplished early next morning. But the fleet after sailing some distance remained weather-bound within sight of both shores for the rest of that day and a great part of the next, so that it was late on the evening of the 29th before it anchored off Burlington. The embarkation of troops and the course of the fleet had been observed by De Rottenburg, and the delay of nearly forty-eight hours enabled Major Maule to reinforce the garrison by a forced march from St. Catharines with 200 men of the 104th. Two parties were landed that night, who took some of the inhabitants by whom they were informed of Maule's arrival. In the morning Scott's whole command, with 250 soldiers and marines, landed under Chapin's guidance near Brant's house, and approached the British position with the apparent intention of making an attack. But as they found it protected by an intrenchment armed with several guns, and a small gunboat cruising in the bay, they abandoned this design and re-embarked before dark, carrying off a few of the inhabitants and some cattle. After midnight, Lieut.-Col. Battersby, who had marched from York the day before upon discovering their destination, arrived with the advance of his "moveable column," and at daybreak Chauncey set sail for that place, which was then left absolutely defenceless. Besides this, the militia had been paroled during the former American occupation, and many of the inhabitants of the vicinity were undeniably disloyal and may have been in communication with the enemy. A month before, Chief Justice Powell had warned the Governor-General that "in the event of any serious disaster to His Majesty's arms, little reliance is to be had on the power of the well disposed to repress and keep down the turbulence of the disaffected, who are very numerous."

Chauncey's schooners entered the bay and landed the troops, who paroled the sick and wounded men in the hospital and broke open the gaol, liberating all the prisoners except three soldiers confined for felony, whom they took away with them. Several hundred barrels of flour were removed from private storehouses to their vessels. While this took place, Commodore Chauncey informed Mr. Strachan and Dr. Powell, who met him as a deputation from the inhabitants, that his visit was intended as a retaliation for the descents of the British squadron on the American coast of the lake, but assured them that none of their houses would be burned. He even apologized for the destruction of the public library at the time of his previous invasion, and stated that he had caused a search to be made throughout his fleet, and that many of the books had been found and would be returned. On the morning of Sunday, August 1st, having been informed by some of the disaffected that military stores had been removed up the Don, they sent a number of boats to ascend that stream. This expedition proved unsuccessful, as the stores had been already taken away by a few of the inhabitants headed by the brothers Playter. At sunset the barracks, woodyard and storehouses on Gibraltar Point were burned, making a flame that was distinctly seen in the British lines about Niagara. On the whole, the invaders behaved well and scarcely molested private property. Elsewhere they do not appear to have exhibited equal moderation, as De Rottenburg wrote from St. Davids

(August 1), "we all day yesterday could perceive smoke from burning houses around the coast."

Battersby's column marched back to York in all haste, but arrived several hours after the enemy's fleet had left the bay. On the 3d Chauncey returned to Niagara and anchored off the mouth of the river, whence he despatched another party of 111 officers and seamen to Lake Erie.

With the exception of a feeble reconnaissance on the 21st July, in which two British dragoons were surprised and taken, Boyd had remained absolutely quiescent within his lines. By throwing the whole body of his Indians into the woods in front of his position De Rottenburg had put an end to all desertion, and the American general complained that it was nearly impossible to obtain any information as to his movements or intentions. On the last day of July, while Chauncey's fleet was entering Toronto Bay, all of the American piquets in front of Niagara were driven in by a general advance and their camp closely reconnoitred, when it was discovered to be strongly fortified, with many cannon mounted and apparently occupied by at least 3000 men under arms. As a matter of fact, Boyd had been recently reinforced by several small detachments, and according to an official return of the 2d of August his division on both sides of the river actually mustered 6635 officers and men of the regular army, exclusive of McClure's battalion of volunteers and Willcocks's command.* But, as the Secretary of War bitterly remarked, "our armies are very great when estimated for pay, but very small in the field." Brigadier-General D. R. Williams, not long since a congressman from South Carolina, and chairman of the Committee on Military Affairs, irreverently known among his colleagues as "Thunder and Lightning Williams," had also arrived as second in command.

On the 24th July, De Rottenburg had issued a district general order referring to the fact that "many farms in the District of Niagara are abandoned by their proprietors or tenants who have joined the enemy," and appointing commissioners "to husband the same and gather in the grain" for the use of the army.† The situation of his division was felt to be one of great peril and entirely dependent on the doubtful result of the struggle for the supremacy of the lake daily expected to begin.

---

* Light Artillery, 481
Dragoons, . . . 241
Artillery, ... 277
Infantry, . . . 5636
} Effectives present, 3835 rank and file.

† The Commissioners named were Richard Hatt, Samuel Hatt, Richard Beaseley, Robert Nelles, Abraham Nelles, Wm. Crooks, Samuel Street, Sr., Thomas Clark, Thomas Dickson, John Warren, Crowell Willson, and Thomas Cummings.

"The fate of this army," wrote Mr. Ridout on the 2d of August, "depends on the fleet. Its positions are so advanced that a retreat will be impossible without losing half the men. The enemy remain cooped up in Fort George, not daring to stir beyond the common. Everything goes on steadily and regularly. Ten thousand of the enemy will not be able to start John Bull out of the Black Swamp ......A large fire seen in the direction of York, supposed to be burnt by the Americans."*

The military chest was empty, and provisions were becoming scarce. The return of Chauncey's fleet with no news of the British squadron so long promised for their relief, had discouraged and intimidated the Indians so much that they could scarcely be kept together. Claus reported, "they are getting tired and impatient. They are dropping off daily, and I fear that in a few days we shall not have many. General De Rottenburg has directed me to purchase everything to be had within fifty miles, but that was not sufficient for fifty men. Tobacco in particular is an article we cannot get." They were given a great "war feast" by the general in person, who states that he had "spared no pains to keep them in good humor."

On the 5th of August his anxiety was much relieved by the arrival of Mr. Hagerman with a message from Yeo, stating that his squadron had been becalmed between the Bay of Quinte and Toronto, and bringing with him a code of signals to distinguish the British positions around Niagara.

On the day that Chauncey returned from his expedition Boyd received letters from the Secretary of War, relieving him from all previous restrictions as to his action. "So long as they had wings and you had only feet, so long as they could be transported, supplied, and reinforced by water and at will," he said, "common-sense as well as military principles put you on the *defensive*. These circumstances changed, the reason of the rule changes with them, and it now becomes your business in concert with the fleet to harass and destroy the enemy wherever you can find them." In a second letter he informed General Boyd that he had just learned that Fort Meigs on the Miami had been lately attacked by a "considerable regular force. This," he added, "must have been drawn from De Rottenburg's corps. His late insolence in pushing his small attacks to the very outline of our works has been intended to mask his weakness produced by this detachment. If, as you say, you can beat him, do it without delay, and if you beat, you must destroy him. There is no excuse for a general who permits a broken enemy to escape and to rally."

The next three days were accordingly spent by Boyd and Chauncey in forming plans and making elaborate preparations for a combined attack. It was intended that the movement should begin on the morning of Sunday, the 8th of August. General Williams was directed to embark on the fleet with one thousand men and land at some favorable point in De Rottenburg's rear to cut off his retreat from the peninsula, while the remainder of the division, advancing simultaneously in two columns by the Queenston and the Lake roads, should assail him in front. General Porter's assistance with the troops stationed at Black Rock and Buffalo was earnestly desired. "The principal force of the enemy being at St. David's," Boyd remarked, "it is thought not advisable for you to descend on this side, but you will please to join us by the other with as great a force of *Indians* as you *can* assemble."

Despite this warning, finding that the Indians collected at Black Rock for the last month, where they had been paid and fed at the public expense, were preparing to abandon him, Porter persuaded them to take part in an inroad into Canada on their own account, which he at first proposed to extend as far as Chippawa, in the hope of effecting a diversion in Boyd's favor. Crossing the river on the morning of the 7th before daylight with 200 regulars and militia and an equal number of Indians, he moved down the Canadian bank until about four miles below Fort Erie, collecting as they went a large herd of cattle and horses found grazing on the commons near the water, and making prisoners of about twenty unarmed inhabitants, among whom were Messrs. Wintemute and Overholt, described as "two noted characters of the revolution." Porter stated that the conduct of his troops in general was excellent, but that "a few unprincipled rascals from our shore with a few Indians strayed off unknown to the officers and plundered several private houses." The Indians were permitted to carry off all the captured cattle, but Porter recommended that the owners should be fully compensated.

At daybreak of the same day, when the arrangements for the proposed attack were nearly complete, Yeo's squadron was descried from Fort George at a distance of about six miles, apparently standing for the head of the lake. Chauncey soon got under way and formed his fourteen ships of war in line of battle. Yeo had but twenty long guns on all his vessels, throwing a broadside of 180 pounds, to oppose sixty-four, throwing 694 pounds at a broadside. But on the other hand he had seventy-two carronades, six of which were sixty-eight pounders, throwing 1194 pounds of shot at a broadside, against Chauncey's fifty, throwing a broadside of 935 pounds. In calm weather or on a light breeze Chauncey had an enormous advantage, as his long guns could wreck the British vessels at a distance which would make their carronades entirely useless. Each of the commanders appears to have known the character of his adversary's armament within a gun or two, and formed his plans accordingly. It was Chauncey's object to engage at a safe distance, while Yeo hoped to force a close action, "though under the guns of their forts." In point of sailing, too, Chauncey's square-rigged vessels were much superior, and were frequently able to take the schooners in tow and bring them into action long before they would have been able to gain a position by their unassisted efforts. But the latter, although fairly good lake vessels, could not manœuvre handily in a gale, and being without bulwarks could scarcely have been fought at all within range of canister, as the men working the guns would have been wholly exposed.

After approaching within four miles, the wind showed signs of shifting into a quarter which might give the British squadron the weather gage, when Chauncey fired a broadside "which did not reach half-way" and returned to his anchorage. On Sunday it was nearly calm, and Yeo directed one of his schooners to approach the enemy's position in the hope of tempting him out into the lake in pursuit. Chauncey sent some of his schooners to sweep out in an effort to cut this vessel off. At two o'clock in the afternoon, a light breeze sprung up and Yeo's squadron stood in to engage, when the schooners again retired. The rest of the day was occupied in similar manœuvres in plain view of the American works, thronged with thousands of eager spectators, and of the British posts of observation along the heights and on the lake shore. During the night the breeze became a gale, and about one o'clock a sudden squall struck two of the largest American schooners—the *Hamilton* of ten and the *Scourge* of nine guns. They careened over, and as they were cleared for action at the time and their guns working on slides, it is supposed that they went to leeward with the shot piled on deck ready for use, and overset these ill-fated vessels within hail of the schooner *Asp*. Their united crews, numbering 118 persons, perished with the exception of sixteen or seventeen, who are said to have been picked up by some of the British vessels then close in pursuit. In the morning Chauncey had regained his anchorage and was seen to receive on board nine boat loads of soldiers, afterwards admitted to amount to 150 men. That day and the next were spent like the two preceding in ineffectual manœuvres. The weather was all that Chauncey could desire for an engagement at long range. Four times he had the wind and bore down to commence the battle, when it suddenly shifted and he declined to allow his adversary the advantage of the weather gage. In the afternoon of the second day the American fleet stood towards the British line favored by a fine breeze, but was becalmed off the British post near the mouth of Twelve Mile Creek. At sunset a south-west breeze blew fresh from the land, giving Yeo the weather gage, and he bore down under press of sail, hoping to pass as rapidly as possible through the zone of fire from their long guns and bring his own carronades to bear before his own ships were disabled. Chauncey stood away and formed his vessels in two parallel lines about 600 yards apart, each line being composed of six vessels, a cable's length distance from each other, the light schooners being to windward and the larger ones with the three square-rigged vessels to leeward. As the British squadron came down in a single line on their larboard quarter the schooners in the weather line were instructed to begin firing as soon as their long 32 and 24 pounders would reach, and gradually bear away and pass through the intervals of the line, still keeping out of range of the British carronades. About eleven Yeo's flagship, the *Wolfe*, leading his squadron and a long distance ahead of all the other vessels, came within range of the hindmost schooners, which opened a brisk but ineffective fire and bore away. They sailed so fast that more than an hour elapsed before the *Wolfe* succeeded in passing them with the intention of engaging the two ships *General Pike* and *Madison*, which led the windward line. During all this time most of the long guns in their squadron had been firing at her with singularly little effect, and all of the schooners in the weather line had passed through or into the second line with exception of the two foremost, the *Julia* and *Growler*, which hauled their wind in succession and shot to windward, either mistaking or disobeying their orders with the intention, as Yeo supposed, of raking his ship while engaged with the rest of the squadron. Yeo's next ship, the *Royal George*, was still two or three miles astern, and the *Wolfe* might have been battered to pieces before she came up. "On coming up with the *Pike* and *Madison*," Yeo wrote, "they put before the wind, firing their stern chase guns. I found it impossible for the remainder of the squadron to get up with them and made between them and two schooners, which I captured." Both of these vessels made a creditable resistance in the chase which followed. The *Growler* was soon disabled by the loss of her bowsprit, but the *Julia*, commanded by Trant, an Irishman, made a desperate attempt to get away and did not surrender until the *Wolfe* almost ran her under. The prizes were stout schooners of about ninety tons—one carrying three, the other two heavy long guns, with crews of forty men each. They were immediately added to the British squadron as the *Hamilton* and *Confiance*. The *Wolfe*, which was the only British vessel that came within range or fired a gun, received no material injury and had not a man hurt.

An officer of the *Pike* has described the action in a letter which was printed about a month afterwards in the *United States Gazette.* "On the 10th at midnight we came within gunshot, everyone in high spirits. The schooners commenced the action with their long guns, which did great execution. At half-past 12 the Commodore fired his broadside and gave three cheers, which was returned from the other ships, the enemy closing fast. We lay by for our opponent, the orders having been given not to fire until she came within pistol shot, though the enemy kept up a constant fire. Every gun was pointed, every match ready in hand, and the red British ensign plainly to be descried by the light of the moon, when, to our utter astonishment, the Commodore wore and stood S. E., leaving Sir James Lucas Yeo to exult in the capture of two schooners and in our retreat, which was certainly a very fortunate one for him."

Chauncey excused his movement, which he described as "edging away two points," by the singular plea that he expected to draw the enemy away from the two schooners he had abandoned and desired to rescue. Cooper considers that his line of battle was well adapted to "draw the enemy down" and "admirable for its advantages and ingenuity." Roosevelt agrees with the British historian James in the judgment that Yeo's conduct was faultless, and admits that he "had attacked a superior force in weather that just suited it and yet had captured two of its vessels without suffering any injury beyond a few shot holes in the sails."

Finding that he was outsailed, Yeo ran into Toronto Bay to refit and man his prizes. "In this narrow water I shall never be able to bring their ships to action," he wrote to the Governor-General, "as I have no vessel which sails sufficiently well to second me.... It concerns me much to find I have such a wary opponent, as it harasses me beyond my strength. I am very unwell, and I believe nothing but the nature of the service keeps me up. I have not closed my eyes for forty-eight hours." Chauncey's vessels were again seen in the lake that day, but it blew hard during the night, and the next morning they had disappeared.

On the 13th Yeo crossed the lake with his squadron increased to eight sail, and anchored at the mouth of the Four-Mile Creek, where he landed some stores and communicated with De Rottenburg. His appearance taken in conjunction with Chauncey's departure alarmed General Boyd so much that he hurriedly summoned the force stationed at Black Rock to come to his assistance, that night if possible. Before it could obey, Yeo had gone down the lake in search of Chauncey, who, after sending two of his schooners into the river, had returned with the remainder of his fleet to Sackett's Harbor, where he arrived on the 13th. He took on board provisions for a five weeks' cruise, sailed the same night or next day, sighted Yeo's squadron off the mouth of the Genesee on its way down the lake, and eventually returned to port after being out only five days.

"We proceeded directly for Sackett's Harbor," said the American officer already quoted, "where we victualled and put to sea the day after our arrival, August 14th. On the 16th we discovered the enemy again, again hurried to quarters, again got clear of the enemy by dint of carrying sail, and returned to Sackett's Harbor. On the 18th we again fell in with the enemy steering for Kingston, and we reached the Harbor on the 19th. This is the result of two cruises, the first of which might by proper guidance have decided in our favor the superiority on the lake and consequently in Canada." For the next nine days Chauncey remained in port, equipping his new schooner and refitting the rest of his vessels. After observing his adversary's retreat into Sackett's Harbor, Yeo returned to Kingston, where he refitted and took in provisions for six or seven weeks with the intention of remaining at the head of the lake. He delayed sailing until the 23rd in order to receive on board fifty men from a troopship laid up at Montreal, who were ordered to join the Lake Erie squadron.

Meanwhile the defection of the Indians had become so alarming that De Rottenburg seized the opportunity afforded by the accidental death of a warrior to visit their camp on the morning of the 7th, and assured them that only the want of wind had detained the squadron. Its appearance an hour or two later quite revived their spirits, and on the 9th Mr. Robert Livingston came in with a body of warriors he had recruited on the north shore of Lake Huron. Livingston was at once sent to the front and "kept the Indians who came with him in constant motion by every day annoying the enemy's piquets, and frequently brought in prisoners and scalps."

A letter from the American camp of August 15th states "that our picket guards during the week have been almost constantly in alarm. On the night of the 13th an attack was made by a pretty formidable force, but flying artillery was sent out and they dispersed. The attacks have been principally made by Indians. The British are supposed to number 2,000 regulars, 500 or 600 Indians, and 300 or 400 Indians. There is no doubt they are short of provisions."

Very early on the morning of the 13th Boyd made an ineffectual attempt to surprise the British outposts on the left. "Our pickets retired this morning." Claus reported to Harvey. "The one in front of Ball's was fired upon by twenty rifles at upwards of 100 yards. They must have been in the bush all night. Some shots were exchanged, but the distance was too great to do any hurt. The one by Secord's did not perceive anything."

The enemy evidently still received information from some disaffected inhabitants. On the 11th August General De Rottenburg acknowledges a letter from Mr. Brenton, the Governor-General's secretary, referring to "traitorous characters who are in league with and give information to the enemy." He recommended the proclamation of martial law as a remedy, and declared that if he could obtain sufficient evidence against "one Peters," an ensign on half-pay, he would try him by court-martial.

On the morning of the 14th General Porter and Major Chapin arrived at Fort Niagara from Black Rock, having made a forced march and crossed the river at the head of 144 Indians and 220 volunteers. Other detachments followed next day, which nearly doubled their number. An agreement had been made with these Indians that they should receive $5 for every private taken prisoner, $30 for a captain, and a proportionate sum for officers of higher rank. They had agreed to abstain from scalping, but seem to have broken this promise at the first opportunity. Chauncey had not returned as General Boyd expected, which in his opinion rendered any important offensive movement impracticable, but he determined to employ these auxiliaries in another attempt to surprise the piquet near Ball's. The force detailed for this enterprise consisted of 300 Indians and volunteers, led by Porter and Chapin, supported by 200 regulars under Major Cummings. A brisk shower of rain caused them to abandon all hope of surprising the piquet, but their approach brought on a hot skirmish, in which, for the first time since the blockade began, they obtained a decided advantage, owing chiefly to the heedlessness of their adversaries.

Colonel Claus described the affair with more than usual detail: "When we got to the advanced piquets more parties were required to be sent out, and our number reduced from upwards of 300 to not more than 50. We had not been here long (advanced piquet) when firing commenced in Ball's fields, to which place I went as quick as possible with the few Indians I had remaining, not supported with or by the troops, and met the Senecas, who, after exchanging some shots, led us into a trap, for in the skirts of the woods there were laying the riflemen and a number of troops. We retired to the first field we engaged them in, and, after some firing, Captain Norton observed that 'it would not do, that we must retire and collect.' That was enough. The word was hardly given when all set from the field, and Major Givins observed to me that we might as well follow. We were then alone in the field at the skirt of the wood. I endeavored to halt them, but all in vain. Our loss was severe this day. I attributed it to dividing us, for our Indians that were detached ran to the spot and met the Senecas, whom they took for our own people. Five were killed, three wounded and ten taken prisoners, besides Captain Lorimier and Livingston the interpreter, who was severely wounded. It was nearly attended with serious consequences. The Western Indians had four of their people killed, and said the Six Nations were the cause of it. Every Indian moved off from their camp some eight or ten miles."

An American eye-witness, whose account appeared in *Poulson's American*, gives some further particulars. "Our force here is about 5,000. We had to-day a brush with the British. Our force was composed of Indians and militia. Two of our allies were brought in dead, and buried with much pomp. Twelve or fifteen white men were brought in prisoners, bound with ropes as if they had been wild beasts. Sundry scalps were exhibited fresh from the heads of the victims. One valuable farm house, with a barn and outhouses, was burnt by our people, and a field of grain set on fire which would not burn. Deserters come in daily."

Livingston was surrounded by the hostile Indians and overpowered after a desperate struggle, in which he received four painful wounds. A blow from a tomahawk destroyed the sight of his right eye, a musket ball lodged in his thigh, where it remained for many months, and he was stabbed in the shoulder and head with a spear. He complained that after being taken he was "refused the least medical aid until his wounds were swarming with worms."

The severity with which the prisoners taken on this occasion were undeniably treated, became the subject of a vigorous protest from De Rottenburg. General Boyd admitted the fact, but carefully disclaimed all personal responsibility. "When the Indians taken prisoners the other day," he replied, "were brought in with ropes around them. I immediately ordered this disgraceful badge to be taken off, and administered to their famished state from my own table. I observed a white man among them, but being told by himself that he was '*an sauvage*,' I conceived his treatment should be similar to the others. The particular rigor he has since experienced was unauthorized by me, and prohibited when the fact came to my knowledge. Since he is acknowledged a British captain, his treatment will be accordingly."

The British Indians took a partial revenge for their losses next day. Another skirmish took place on the Ball farm, which continued with the usual amount of firing and whooping for three

killed in '37 at Montgomery's Tavern,) by the lake road to surprise piquets one and two. Packs and all other encumbrances were left in camp. Lieutenant-Colonel O'Neil of the 19th Light Dragoons, with thirty troopers of his regiment, followed, and, supported by the whole body of Indians, covered the advance on the village. The attack began shortly after daybreak, while the fog hung heavy on the plain. All the piquets were surprised by a sudden rush nearly at the same instant, and a considerable number of prisoners taken. Captain FitzGerald of the 49th, in leading the attack on the piquet upon the Queenston Road, fell with a gunshot wound, which subsequently caused the amputation of his leg. In the confusion which followed, Captain Davenport of the 16th U. S. I., who commanded this post, escaped with most of his men, even carrying off some of his assailants as prisoners. Captain Delano of the 23rd U. S. I., retiring with the remnant of another piquet, stumbled upon FitzGerald as he was being removed from the field, and carried him into his own lines. Captain Vandalsen of the 15th U. S. I., in charge of the piquet near Butler's house, also succeeded in effecting his retreat with slight loss. Lieutenant-Colonel Harvey, who had been detailed to reconnoitre the works, dashed gallantly into the village at the head of the dragoons, scouring the streets as far as the Presbyterian Church, from the steeple of which he secured a complete view of all their intrenchments, which bristled with cannon and were crowded with men. As soon as the firing was heard and their outposts were seen flying for shelter across the commons, two columns, led by General Williams and Colonel James Miller, with two field-pieces, advanced to their relief, and their light troops began a brisk fire out of the windows of houses and from behind fences and garden walls, while the batteries of the camp were turned upon the village. Eventually these troops, which had been instructed to act strictly on the defensive, retired into their intrenchments, which were then closely reconnoitred. "No provocation could induce the American army to leave their places of shelter," Prevost wrote to Lord Bathurst, "and venture into the field, where alone I could hope to contend with it successfully. Having made a display of my force in vain, a deliberate retreat ensued, without a casualty. I am now satisfied that Fort George is not to be reduced, strengthened and supported as it is by Fort Niagara, without more troops, the co-operation of the fleet, and a battering train. To accomplish this object a double operation becomes necessary. Fort Niagara must be invested, and both places be attacked at the same moment."

A letter in the New York *Evening Post* relates that "on the 24th of August the enemy made their appearance at our advanced post No. 6, and on being challenged, replied 'deserters.' The centinel replied 'pass deserters,' and was taken. The other centinel ran in and warned the guard, who fired and dispersed. The arms of the British were unloaded, wishing to take them by surprise, and only 17 out of 47 of whom the guard consisted were taken. In this skirmish Captain FitzGerald of the 49th was wounded. A party afterwards went out and captured him with two men, who were carrying him away. Before we had time to support our other posts, they were driven in (Nos. 1 to 5) with equal loss, and the enemy penetrated to the very centre of the town of Newark, and skirting the woods in our front rested his right on the Niagara, occupying our post No. 6, his left on the lake, and his centre within view and gunshot of our works."

Lieutenant Jones and a private of the 49th were wounded, two men of the 104th were killed and three wounded, in the course of the day's operations. The number of prisoners taken is variously stated by British authorities from fifty to seventy, and belonged to at least five different regular regiments.* General Boyd at first reported that his loss was trifling, but five days later admitted that it was much greater than he had supposed, having learned that there were five men killed and twenty-seven missing. Besides Captain FitzGerald, he stated that six privates were taken prisoners by his troops, and concluded his despatch with the absurd remark, "his force is withdrawn out of our reach into his stronghold."

An attack upon Boyd's formidable entrenchments with the very inferior force at his command would have been little less than madness, yet the spirits of the loyal inhabitants had been so much elated by a series of remarkable and unhoped-for successes that many were ready to censure the Governor-General for having declined to undertake it. A writer of the present day heedlessly condemns the reconnoissance on the assumption that "at the time no explanation of its design was offered, and it has remained to this day unexplained and inexplicable."

General Boyd's determination not to be drawn from the defensive seemed to have caused similar dissatisfaction and criticism among his troops, which as usual was readily repeated by the newspapers.

"General Boyd and Major Chapin have quarreled," says a letter from Geneva of September 3d, in the New York *Commercial Advertiser*. "Major Chapin has discharged the Indians who were under him. The cause of this disagreement was the general not supporting the major when the British made an attack and drove in the American piquets stationed at Newark. The major finding

* 2nd Dragoons, 6th, 13th, 16th and 23rd U. S. Infantry.

the British too strong for him, sent for a reinforcement of 700 men with two field-pieces. No answer being returned, Major Chapin sent for half the number and one field-piece. This was not granted. The consequence was that the British out-flanked our men, killing and wounding many, and obtained possession of the town, and from the Presbyterian church steeple they had a fine view of our encampment. The British kept possession of the town a very short time—long enough, however, for those who had been refused permission to depart from thence to leave it, which they did with shouts of joy."

" The agreement with the Indians allows them $5 for each private taken and $30 for a captain, and so on in proportion to their rank. They are not allowed any sum for scalps, nor are they permitted to scalp any white person, but they have taken the liberty to scalp the British Indians.

" A few days since a private dwelling house was set on fire by our troops in Newark. The next night the Presbyterian Church was destroyed the same way. General Boyd says it was by Major Chapin's troops, and Major Chapin declares it to have been done by the regulars."

After the demonstration of the 24th of August, several days seem to have passed without noteworthy incident, except that Captain Gordon of the Royal Scots, in moving along the line of outposts lost his way in a fog and entered the American lines, where he was taken prisoner by Thomas Gray, a private of the 15th U. S. infantry, who was rewarded by the gift of a silver cup " with a suitable inscription," from General Boyd.

After being becalmed for two days near the Ducks, Yeo sailed up the lake without seeing anything of the enemy's fleet. He sent a transport loaded with provisions into York and two others conveying men, guns and naval stores for the Lake Erie squadron to Burlington, and on the 27th appeared off Niagara with eight sail. One of his schooners ran in so close to the mouth of the river as to exchange shots with the American batteries. Next day he captured the schooner *Mary*, of Oswego, on its way to Fort Niagara with flour and lumber for the army, and crossed the lake to York. On the 29th he returned, and after landing Lieut.-Colonel Bruyeres, of the Royal Engineers, who was sent to conduct the siege operations, and a party of artillerymen, at the mouth of the Four Mile Creek, sailed for a cruise along the American shore in search of their convoys of provisions.

By this time the heat had become almost unendurable, and sickness had vastly increased. " The weather is intensely warm," De Rottenburg wrote on the 30th, "and everybody is more or less affected by it. Colonel Stewart, Major Plenderleath, Major

Williams, FitzGibbon and a great number of others are laid up with the lake fever. We are in great need of medicines."

"Last evening our fleet came over," says Mr. Ridout, "and proceeded to the Twelve-Mile Creek on the American side to intercept supplies by water, which the Yankees have daily received. Great victory in Spain (Vittoria). De Watteville's regiment is very much wanted here. The 49th are reduced to about 370 men. This morning three companies, amounting to about 75, have arrived from Burlington: 50 Royal Artillery have joined by the fleet.

"By what I can learn, Sir George's presence here is very little sought for: he has no idea of attacking the Americans on their own ground. The summit of his wishes is to recover Fort George and remain there. The great officers say this army will be ruined by petty affairs. Some heavy cannon have arrived at Burlington. The army have been these two days out of whiskey. There is a good deal of ague among the men. The 8th have neither blankets nor great coats, but a large supply have arrived."*

It was then seriously proposed to bring a division of 2000 men under Major-General Stovin with a siege train of fourteen guns in the squadron from Kingston, land them at the Four-Mile Creek on the American side, invest Fort Niagara and begin a regular siege on both sides of the river. But this could not be done with safety so long as the American fleet was able to contest the command of the lake.

Having equipped and manned the new schooner *Sylph* and taken on board two regiments of infantry, Chauncey had sailed from Sackett's Harbor on the 28th of August. On the 3rd September he appeared off Niagara and ran into the river during the night. Yeo, being then off York, left a number of empty transports which he was conveying to Kingston for the conveyance of the siege-train to pursue their voyage alone, crossed the lake and anchored off the mouth of the Four Mile Creek on the evening of the 4th.

De Rottenburg had already removed his headquarters to the left in hope of beginning the siege as soon as Yeo returned, but his chief engineer then declared that it would be impossible to drive the American fleet out of the river and commence operations without mortars. Two ten-inch guns mounted on Brown's Point, he said, would be sufficient. "If the fleet should leave me," De Rottenburg wrote, "I cannot hold my position with so powerful a fleet in the river. If I cannot get heavy artillery I cannot attempt anything with only six field-pieces and howitzers. I have now at the Twelve-Mile Creek and at York over 500 sick." By this time nearly the

---

* Edgar, Ten Years of Upper Canada, p. 210.

whole of his Indians, except those from the Grand River, had returned to their homes, and desertion had again become alarmingly frequent among the regular troops. Two men of the 8th, four of the Canadian Voltigeurs and three of the 49th had deserted in a single day.

"We have changed our headquarters to the lake side," writes Mr. Ridout. "The encampment here is very beautiful, and is formed of the 8th and 104th and part of the 89th and 100th Regiments, consisting of 2000 men. They lie upon the edge of the woods, having large clearings in front, and the main road crossing the camp by Mr. Addison's, where the general stays. Very few troops are left in St. Davids......The army is getting very sickly. There are more than 400 sick, and a great number of officers. York is considered the healthiest place for the hospitals. We cannot stand this daily diminution of strength ten days longer. Our fleet is just coming over from York—I suppose with De Watteville's regiment. Four of the Glengarrys deserted yesterday, and four American dragoons deserted to us."

But great as the amount of sickness in the blockading force may appear, the ravages of disease were vastly more serious in the American camp. A large body of men had been practically shut up within it for three months. Their encampment was badly policed, heaps of rubbish and refuse were allowed to accumulate everywhere and a horrible stench rose from the sinks, to the neglect of which the surgeons ascribed much of the ill health of the troops. With the exception of a few hot days in the beginning of June, the whole of that month and the first ten days in July had been unusually wet and cool. Then a "severe and unrelenting drought" set in, which lasted for almost two months. The village of Niagara intercepted the breeze from the lake, while the unbroken forest stretching for many miles southward along the eastern bank kept the wind away from those quarters. The pitiless midsummer sun beat down upon their camp until it glowed like a furnace. "Thus having been wet for nearly a month," says Dr. Lovell, "our troops were exposed for six or seven weeks to intense heat during the day and at night to a cold and chilly atmosphere, in consequence of the fog arising from the lake and river. The enemy's advance being within a short distance of the camp, the details for duty were large, and skirmishes taking place at the piquets every morning the soldiers were for a length of time stationed at the several works for several hours before daylight, and thus exposed to the effects of a cold, damp atmosphere at the time when the system is most susceptible to morbid impressions."

The detestable quality of the provisions furnished by the contractors was another fruitful source of disease. Much of the bread was unfit to be eaten. In some cases the flour had become mouldy, in others it had been so largely adulterated with ground plaster of paris that it could be detected by the eye as well as by its excessive weight.

From less than seven hundred at the beginning of August the number of sick regularly increased to 1165 rank and file out of 4587 three weeks later. Nor did this return represent the true extent of their losses by disease. "From an estimation of numbers sick in the general and regimental hospitals," said Dr. Mann, their surgeon-in-chief, "it was my persuasion that but little more than one-half of the army were capable of duty at one period during the summer months. The officers suffered equally with the rank and file......There was one regiment on the frontiers which at one time counted 900 strong, but was reduced by a total want of good police to less than 200 fit for duty in the course of two months. ......At one time 340 of this regiment were in hospitals, besides a large number reported sick in camp......Half of the medical staff attached to the regiments were also unable to perform their duty. Of seven surgeon's mates attached to the hospital department, one died and three had leave of absence by reason of indisposition, the other three were for a short period sick. So general was the sickness that the few remaining surgeons could not do full justice to their patients......Deserters from the British army, of whom some hundreds came to our posts, exhibited marks of high health, while our soldiers were pallid and emaciated."

The number of deaths was not great, the only one of note among them being Colonel John Chrystie, the senior officer of that rank in the division.

Although great efforts had been made during the whole year to increase the American regular army by offering bounties and other inducements to enlist, private information received by the British commanders indicated that recruiting scarcely kept pace with their losses.

Porter and Chapin appear to have retired from the American camp with the greater part of their force about the 27th August, and after remaining a few days at Lewiston, returned to Black Rock, where they began recruiting for another "excursion." A number of their Indians still continued with General Boyd.

Wilkinson, the new commander of the "Army of the Centre," arrived at Sackett's Harbor on the 20th August with the intention of making Kingston the first point of attack, and with this object of bringing down the greater part of Boyd's division in the fleet, at the time when Yeo and De Rottenburg were actually contemplating a similar movement of its garrison up the lake to assist in the reduction of the forts at the mouth of the Niagara. Wilkinson became alarmed when he learned about a week later that Prevost had gone westward, and sent a warning message to "prevent his playing tricks with Boyd." Then, in a highly characteristic vein, he began to cast up his chances of success. "What an awful crisis have I reached! If Sir George beats Boyd, and Sir James, Chauncey, my prospects are blasted and the campaign will, I fear, be lost. If Sir George beats Boyd, and Chauncey, Sir James, Kingston may yet be ours, but should both knights be beaten, and our quartermaster find transports in season (of which I have fears, as I have found next to none here,) then we shall certainly winter in Montreal if not discomfited by some act of God."

On the 4th of September he arrived at Fort Niagara to find Chauncey's fleet blockaded in the river and "Sir James Yeo with the British squadron vaporing in front of it." This state of affairs continued until the evening of the 7th, when a light land breeze enabled the American vessels to enter the lake again. For three days both fleets remained in sight without firing a gun, and each manœuvering in the hope of securing the weather gage, at a distance varying from four to eight miles. On the 11th they had disappeared, and on the afternoon of that day the British squadron was becalmed near the mouth of the Genesee. Chauncey, with a light wind, succeeded in getting within range of his numerous long guns in weather that just suited his vessels. Before sailing, the *Sylph* had been armed with four long thirty-two pounders mounted on circles between the masts, avowedly in the hope of "bringing down some of the enemy's spars." She carried besides, six long sixes in broadside and is said to have taken on board some other long guns while at Niagara. Consequently Chauncey's superiority at long range was even greater than before. But his crews had been much weakened by sickness, and deserters reported that his vessels were decidedly short-handed when they entered the river. He endeavored to make up for this by taking on board a body of riflemen to act as marines. He judiciously made the most of his opportunity by keeping out of range of his adversary's carronades and firing deliberately in perfect security. "We remained in this mortifying situation five hours," said Yeo, "having only six guns in all the squadron that would reach the enemy (not a carronade being fired.)" Mr. Roosevelt considers it a "proof of culpable incompetency" that he did not substitute some of his long guns for his carronades, but as Yeo's whole career proves him ready-witted and resourceful, there were probably excellent reasons for not adopting so obvious an expedient as this may seem to a landsman. At sunset a breeze sprung up from the westward and Yeo made for the False Duck Islands, under which he believed that his antagonist would be unable to retain the weather gage. Chauncey declined to follow him, alleging that Amherst Bay is "so little known to our pilots and said to be so full of shoals that they are unwilling to take me there." It must have required no little audacity to write, "I am much disappointed that Sir James refused to fight me as he was so much superior in point of force, both in guns and men, having upwards of twenty guns more than we have and heaves a greater weight of shot."

The fire of his heavy guns had been attended with surprisingly little result, Midshipman Ellery and three seamen were killed and seven seamen wounded on Yeo's ship, and the brig *Melville* received a shot so far below the water line that in order to plug it all her guns had to be run in on one side and out on the other, but not a spar was lost or scarcely even injured Having thus "exhausted his naval tactics in endeavouring to obtain the weather gage," Yeo returned to Kingston on the 15th, "almost chased" into port, to the keen disappointment of the Governor-General, who had hoped for a "decided advantage."

The booming of the cannonade had been heard far inland by the New York militia gathering to march to Niagara, and rumors of a great battle spread fast. They soon came to Wilkinson's ears, and being as "wild and extravagant as they are inconsistent and contradictory," made him sigh for "an end of this uncertainty, which damps our exertions and retards our measures."

On the 6th of September a British foraging party engaged in cutting a field of oats on Ball's farm was attacked by American Indians, and Claus and Captain Wm. J. Kerr went to their rescue with some of the Six Nations. A party of the Glengarry Light Infantry also advanced, and American riflemen came out to cover the retreat of their Indians. Firing continued for nearly three hours, before the latter were finally driven in. Two of the American Oneidas were killed and the same number wounded, while Claus had two Mohawks wounded and a drunken Cayuga warrior ran into the hands of the enemy. One of his Tuscaroras, who was very drunk, ran forward in pursuit near the close of the skirmish and drew their fire upon him, by which he was killed, and a young Delaware, who attempted to go to his relief and shot a white man in the act of scalping him, received two wounds. The Six Nations and their leaders were thanked in general orders for their good conduct in this encounter, which was the only one that took place for several days.

One of General Wilkinson's first measures was to issue an address to the Six Nations residing within the United States, calling upon them to "organize, embody, and assemble as speedily as possible at the most convenient place" and send a deputation of chiefs to confer with him. Three hundred and fifty eventually responded to this summons and were joined by two hundred of the Oneida and Stockbridge tribes from near the centre of the State.* A brigade of 2,650 New York militia had been ordered to assemble at Lewiston on the 7th September, but it was nearly three weeks later before it actually arrived, and did not then muster quite 2000 men.

Two unimportant incursions were in the meantime undertaken by the volunteer force assembled near Buffalo. On the 14th September Chapin crossed the lake with fifty men in the hope of surprising a militia guard stationed at Zavitz's mills near the Sugar Loaf, but found that Colonel Warren had been warned of their approach and withdrawn it into the interior. Three days later General Porter landed eight miles below Fort Erie and moved up the Canadian bank to the ferry without opposition.

During all this time De Rottenburg continued to lose heavily by desertion. Every account from the American camp refers to the constant stream of deserters that were coming in, sometimes as many as seven or eight in a day and never less than two. General Wilkinson himself states sixty-five arrived in the first sixteen days of September, and that he had lost barely six. Yet he found it necessary to hang one of his own men as an example. Another officer, writing on the 13th, estimates that nearly 300 men had deserted from the British since the American army had entered Canada.

Many of the inhabitants had become so much intimidated by the severity of the enemy in the deportation of numbers of the loyalists and destruction of their buildings, that they were unwilling to take employment even as teamsters or mechanics, and the Governor-General eventually found it necessary to publish a special order protesting against "the unjustifiable practice of the United States in paroling unarmed and peaceable citizens," and stating that "several subjects had been deterred from accepting employment in their several callings as mechanics, and otherwise, for fear of being punished for violating their parole." He asserted that paroles could only be considered binding on persons actually engaged in military services or found with arms in their hands, and that a parole when lawfully taken could only extend to military service in the garrison or the field and would not preclude them from performing their ordinary duties as subjects or from the exercise of their civil occupations,

* The number of Indians in the employment of the United States on this frontier must have been considerable. As late as 1862, the claims for pensions were allowed of 83 Indians of the Alleghany Reservation, 218 of the Cattaraugus Reservation, two of Cornplanter's, 86 of the Onondaga Nation, 11 of the Oneida Nation, 17 of the Tuscarora Nation, or 415 in all.

and that in the event of any such persons being treated with undue severity, he would retaliate in like manner. It was added that there was strong reason to believe that in several instances the paroles so given had been sought by the persons themselves as affording a means of evading their military and other duties, and that all "such useless and disaffected characters" would be sent out of the country to the enemy as prisoners of war to remain until exchanged."

On the 19th of September, having remained in port four days, Sir James Yeo again sailed from Kingston, having under convoy seven small vessels loaded with supplies and siege guns for De Rottenburg. "The centre division of the army in Upper Canada," the Governor-General said in his instructions, "has long been in the singular position of investing a superior force; it is much weakened by disease and desertion, and its position rendered critical by the temporary naval ascendency of the enemy. The policy of the American commanders is to protract the final decision, in the expectation of depriving me of the means of forwarding supplies, as it is well known the state of the country will only admit of their being transported by water......This position was adopted and has been maintained in the expectation that with the co-operation of your squadron a combined attack could be made upon Fort George. You are to proceed to the head of the lake, affording a sufficient convoy to the small vessels containing those stores and supplies of which the army is in most pressing want. On your arrival at the head-quarters of the centre division, you are to consult with General De Rottenburg upon the eligibility of a rapid forward movement upon Fort George, bringing up in battery at the same time the heavy ordnance, mortars, and howitzers now embarked. The attack to be supported by your squadron. If this proves too hazardous for the squadron in case of the the enemy appearing upon the lake, to state it to General De Rottenburg, who will evacuate the position he now occupies, and, having assisted him in this, to do what is possible to ensure ascendency on the lake. The flotilla of transports to be kept employed as long as the weather will admit, in the conveying of stores from Kingston for the right and centre divisions of the army."

Instructions had already been forwarded to De Rottenburg, authorizing him to retire as far as Burlington if he thought proper, but he had replied that he would only do this in case of absolute necessity, as he must then sacrifice the resources of the country in his rear. He was now directed to maintain his position as long as it was prudent, "although exposed to a lamentable prevalence of disease and desertion and the increasing numbers and resources of the enemy. The land operations depend almost entirely on successes of the fleet, but to have relinquished one foot of ground on which we so proudly stand would have lost all our wavering friends and have proved destructive of our Indian allies."

When these orders reached him, De Rottenburg was reduced to the verge of despair. " What with sickness and desertion," he wrote on the 17th of September, " I am now almost *au bout de mon latin*, and my situation daily becomes more desperate. More than 1,000 men are laid up with disease, and officers in still greater proportion. Daily five or six villains go off. There is no thoroughly healthy spot to retire to as far as York. Burlington is as bad as here. The fever and ague rages, and the inhabitants are as sickly as the soldiers. If you cannot send me fresh troops the country will be lost for want of hands to defend it. If I am attacked and forced back the sick will be lost for want of conveyance."

About the same time, Mr. Ridout states that " desertion has come to such a pass that eight or ten men go off daily....Their deserters come in every day. They say that 4,000 men are at Fort George. The other day a Yankee picket shot two of our deserters dead. One of the 49th attempted to swim over by Queenston, but was killed by the sentry."

There can be no doubt that the distressed state of the blockading army was perfectly well-known to the enemy, and it is astonishing that he should have abstained from an attack, when success must have seemed all but certain. "If the enemy's sick list amounts to one thousand four hundred out of three thousand," the Secretary of War said to Wilkinson, "the enemy can undertake nothing with effect." When this was written, a return of the division at Fort George showed that it numbered 4587 rank and file, of whom 3422 were fit for duty.

Yet De Rottenburg gallantly prepared for the continuance of the blockade. When the autumnal rains fairly set in his position in and about the Black Swamp would no longer be tenable, and he proposed to remove his quarters to the high ground extending from Queenston to Chippawa.

For about ten days after General Wilkinson's arrival at Fort George he was confined to his bed, according to his own statement, by a "severe and unremitting malady," which caused "much depression of the head and stomach." Others roundly asserted that he was suffering from the effects of drink. On the 16th he announced that he had "escaped from his pallet with a giddy head and trembling hand," but nothing had been heard from Chauncey since his departure, and the result of the naval action was still unknown. The militia had not yet arrived, but "the Indians," he said, "enter into our views with zeal, and I expect a corps of at least five hundred in eight days." Estimating his own effective force at 3400 and that of the British blockading him at 1600, he inquired: "Shall I make a sweep of them or not, at the hazard of the main object?"

On the 19th, a number of schooners and large boats arrived from Oswego for the conveyance of Boyd's division. Chauncey had sailed from Sackett's Harbor on the 17th, but was driven back by a storm. Next day he sailed again, and sighted the British squadron with its convoy on its way up the lake. But he made no attempt to intercept it, for the Secretary of War had come to Sackett's Harbor on purpose to supervise the operations of the army, and had said: "Let not the great objects of the campaign be hazarded by running after Yeo. These accomplished, his race is run. Kingston or the point below seized, all above perishes, because the tree is then girdled."

Yeo for his part, encumbered with transports and siege guns, was only too glad to pursue his course unmolested. The American fleet arrived at Niagara on the 23rd, and two days later 1,500 men were embarked, but a strong easterly gale prevented them from sailing. On the 26th the weather again became fair and the troops were in readiness, but Wilkinson had learned by that time that " the tantalizing Sir James Yeo was in shore with his fleet on the evening of the 24th about twenty-eight miles east of York." Chauncey sent two light vessels to reconnoitre, which reported seeing the British squadron in Toronto Bay. The American fleet of eleven ships of war sailed out of the river early on the morning of the 28th, and shortly afterwards the British squadron was descried beating across the lake. Any movement of troops down the lake in the face of a hostile squadron was out of the question, and Chauncey went out to meet it. Yeo lay to about twelve miles away and awaited the attack. Again Chauncey had the wind in his favor and was able to choose his distance. Firing began about noon, and within a quarter of an hour a lucky shot from one of the *Pike's* long guns carried away the main topmast of the *Wolfe*, which in its fall brought down the mizzen topmast and main yard. The flag-ship became quite unmanageable on a wind, and to save her Yeo was obliged to put before a strong gale, which had begun to blow, towards Burlington Bay. His flight was nobly covered by the *Royal George*, commanded by Captain (afterwards Sir W. H.) Mulcaster. " This vessel," says Mr. Cooper, " kept yawing athwart the English Commodore's stern and delivering her broadsides in a manner to extort exclamations of delight from the American fleet."* A running fight was continued in this manner for up-

---

* History of the U. S. Navy, vol. II, p. 374

wards of two hours, until within about ten miles of the head of the lake, when Chauncey abandoned the pursuit. One of the bow guns on his flag ship had burst, tearing up the top-gallant forecastle, dismounting a pivot gun mounted there and killing or wounding no less than twenty-two men. Five others had been injured by shot. The confusion incident upon such an accident was no doubt sufficient to justify hauling off, but in addition to this the *Pike* had lost her main topmast, her bowsprit, fore and main masts were badly wounded, her rigging and sails cut up, and several round shot had pierced her hull below the water line, which kept all her pumps going. The *Governor Tompkins* was disabled by the loss of her foremast, and both the *Madison* and *Oneida* had their spars cut up by round shot.

The foretopmast of the *Royal George* fell just as she came to anchor, but the British squadron does not seem to have lost a man. Two days were occupied in refitting, during which Chauncey kept the lake, being in sight much of the time. Yeo was intensely annoyed at the unusual experience of having to run from an enemy before a man was hurt, and was overheard by his pilot to say to Mulcaster: "If we were on the high seas I would risk an action at all hazards, because if I were beaten I could only lose the squadron, but to lose it on this lake would involve the loss of the country. The salvation of the western army depends on our keeping open their communications."* This affair was ever after known in his squadron as the " Burlington Races."

About two hours after the American fleet had sailed to meet Yeo, a numerous flotilla of Durham boats was observed to come out of the river and anchor at the mouth of a creek beyond Fort Niagara. The movements of the contending ships of war were watched with the deepest anxiety by the officers of both armies until they went out of sight. The Americans were able to "distinguish the *Pike* firing both her batteries, and frequently enveloped in smoke." Captain O'Conor, one of Yeo's officers who was ashore with De Rottenburg, took a station on Queenston Heights, whence he saw the *Wolfe* lose her topmasts and the entire squadron run into Burlington Bay. Before dark all the American boats re-entered the river, as General Wilkinson feared to attempt the voyage without a convoy. He peevishly complained that he "had difficulties, perplexities and anxieties sufficient to discompose a saint."

The movement of troops and artillery across the river could not fail to be observed by De Rottenburg, and deserters assured him that Sackett's Harbor was their destination. This information seems to have prompted him to undertake a counter demonstration

* Coffin, The War and its Moral, p. 167.

on the morning of the following day. An order was issued for all the troops to be in readiness to move at an instant's notice, tents were struck, and wagons loaded. A deserter then made his escape to Fort George, bearing this note addressed to Major V. Huyck, 13th U. S. Infantry : "Every movement of the army is either an advance or retreat; about 2270 strong." This opportune bit of information was written by Noah Hopkins, a saddler at Queenston, who was the son-in-law of an American colonel, and seems to have been constantly employed as a spy. He was afterwards detected and hung for treasonable practices, on the 20th July, 1814. The intelligence brought by this man caused something like a panic in Wilkinson's camp, but finally two strong columns marched out to oppose the attack if one was intended, or profit by the retreat. As neither took place, they returned to their quarters without doing anything.

On the 1st of October Chauncey returned to Niagara, still watched by Yeo, who anchored at the mouth of the Twelve Mile Creek. Leaving about 1,800 regulars, militia and Indians to occupy the forts and camp, Wilkinson finally embarked the remainder of his forces and set off on his long projected expedition. Yeo's opportune appearance on the 7th of September had caused a delay of eighteen days; his return on the 20th had been responsible for the loss of another week, when time and fair weather was of the utmost importance. Although he had gained no brilliant success and had finally been compelled to seek safety in flight, his services to the army had been most meritorious and effective. "In executing his orders," even Mr. Cooper is constrained to admit, "the English Commodore, who was an officer of rare merit, manifested great steadiness, self-denial and address, and the skill and boldness with which he manœuvred received the applause of his enemies."*

The long beleaguerment of the American camp was now about to close abruptly. As soon as General Wilkinson's purpose was placed beyond doubt De Rottenburg despatched to the defence of Kingston three of his strongest regiments and prepared to follow himself, leaving Vincent to maintain the blockade as long as possible. The defeat of the British squadron on Lake Erie was followed by General Procter's retreat from Detroit and his total rout on the Thames. Parties of New York militia raided the frontier between Fort Erie and the Falls, and large bodies of these troops were seen assembling at Lewiston and Fort Niagara.

"The Americans have possession of our side as far down as Samuel Street's, and have plundered all the loyal inhabitants of their property, " writes Mr. Ridout on the 2nd October. "The

---

* Naval Hist. of U. S., II, 381.

greater part of the settlement being Dutch Mennonites, are friendly to the enemy and assist them in everything. We have lately taken a number of their waggons.

"We expect some serious movement every hour, as the enemy are in great force at Fort George.... We are driving all the cattle from this part of the district towards the head of the lake. The Chippawa and Short Hills country is stript of cattle, and to-day they are driving them from the vicinity of the camps. The waggons stand ready loaded with the baggage which moves in the rear."[*]

On the 6th there was a lively skirmish, in which the light company of the Royal Scots drove Chapin's volunteers through the streets of the village and entered it in pursuit. Colonel Scott, who was in command at Fort George, turned his artillery on the houses, when the Scots hastily retreated. They lost one prisoner and five wounded, while Chapin admitted losing six men killed and ten wounded, besides some prisoners.

Three days afterwards, when De Rottenburg had gone as far as the Twelve Mile Creek on his way to Kingston, he met the panic-stricken adjutant of General Procter's staff, who falsely reported that the whole of his division had been captured, and that the American mounted riflemen were rapidly advancing upon Burlington from the scene of the disaster. This story caused an immediate retreat in much hurry and confusion, although, fortunately for them, there was no attempt at pursuit. As it was, a considerable quantity of stores were destroyed and the sick and wounded suffered dreadfully. "Upwards of 300 men upon the road," says an eyewitness, "and waggons loaded with miserable objects stuck fast in mudholes, broken down and unable to ascend the hills, and the men too ill to stir hand or foot."

The audacity and success with which a protracted blockade had been maintained by a greatly inferior force is indisputable. From the 14th of July until the beginning of October the main army of invasion from which so much had been expected had not only been hemmed in and held in check, but kept in constant terror of attack, while it wasted away with desertion and disease.

"The army at Fort George," says Dr. Mann, who was with it all the time, "consumed the most eligible season of the summer and autumn for effective service cooped within the narrow limits of a few acres of land by a force of the enemy not exceeding one-half of its strength, and, under a constant apprehension of an attack, placed itself wholly in a state of defence. This apparent pusillanimity or want of confidence on the part of the army emboldened the

---

[*] Edgar, Ten Years of Upper Canada.

enemy to insult by repeated attacks upon its advanced piquets night after night......This *petit guerre* kept the army in constant alarm and subjected the troops to vexatious fatigues, unremitted duty, and multiplied exposures, which prevented them from taking their necessary repose......When an enemy exhibits great military talents, we are disposed to allow him all the credit due in a martial point of view, even when by artful deceptions and judicious management with a force inferior he was enabled to apparently check the offensive operations of our army and compel it to place itself in a position entirely defensive."*

* Medical History of the War, pp. 94-6.

CHRONOLOGY.

1813.

May 27 The British evacuate Fort George and retreat to Beaver Dams.
"   28 The Americans advance to Queenston and St. Davids. Colonel Preston occupies Fort Erie. Vincent retires to the Forty.
"   29 General Chandler returns to Niagara to embark on the fleet.
"   30 Colonel Preston issues his proclamation.
"   31 Vincent retires to Burlington.
June 1 General Winder advances to the Fifteen.
"   2 He advances to the Thirty.
"   3 He advances to the Forty. General Chandler marches to his support.
"   4 Chandler arrives at the Forty.
"   5 The Americans advance to Stoney Creek and drive in the British piquets.
"   6 Action at Stoney Creek. The Americans retreat to the Forty. General Lewis is instructed to assume command of the division.
"   7 Lewis arrives at the Forty. The British fleet is seen from Fort George, and General Dearborn send orders to Lewis to retreat. The British squadron arrives at the Forty.
"   8 Sir J. Yeo cannonades the American camp at the Forty, sails to Burlington, and returns. He pursues and captures the American boats. The Americans retreat and Major Evans occupies their camp.
"   9 Major Dennis advances to the Twenty. The Americans evacuate Fort Erie and Queenston. The Lincoln militia take possession of Queenston.
"   10 Vincent advances to the Forty. Skirmish at the Ten. The Americans remove their armed vessels from Black Rock.
"   12 Yeo sails from the Forty, and takes two American vessels at Eighteen-Mile Creek. British piquets advance again to St. Catharines.
"   14 Sir George Prevost publishes his counter-proclamation.
"   15 Yeo lands at the Genesee.
"   16 He arrives at Kingston and sails again. The Lady Murray taken by the Americans. FitzGibbon occupies DeCew's house. Chapin enters Canada.
"   17 Yeo menaces Oswego.
"   19 Yeo lands at Sodus. Chapin arrives at Fort George. Dearborn orders arrest of the loyal inhabitants.
"   20 Yeo returns to the Forty. DeHaren and Ducharme arrive with reinforcements. Bisshopp advances to the Twenty. Dearborn writes for Indians.
"   22 Skirmish at Lundy's Lane.
"   23 Colonel Boerstler advances to Queenston.
"   24 Action at Beaver Dams.
"   25 British Indians retire to the Forty.
"   28 Vincent advances to St. Catharines.
"   29 British outposts advanced to the Four-Mile Creek. Yeo returns to Kingston. De Rottenburg assumes command.
July 1 The British occupy St. Davids.
"   4 Fort Schlosser taken.
"   5 Skirmish near Fort Erie. Western Indians arrive. The Six Nations have a "talk" at Queenston.
"   7 The British occupy Fort Erie.
"   8 Skirmish at Butler's Farm. Indian council at the Twelve. British scouts cross the river near Black Rock.
"   11 Attack on Black Rock. Skirmish at Ball's farm.
"   14 General Dearborn retires from the command.
"   15 Arrival of the remainder of the Royals and 104th.
"   17 De Rottenburg removes his headquarters to St. Davids. Skirmish in Ball's fields.
"   20 A squadron of the 19th Dragoons arrives.
"   21 Indian Council at the Cross Roads.
"   23 American fleet sails from Sackett's Harbor.
"   25 Indian Council at the Cross Roads.
"   27 American fleet arrives at Fort George and embark troops.
"   30 Americans land at Burlington.

1813.

July	31	Americans land at York. Yeo sails from Kingston. De Rottenburg reconnoitres Fort George.
Aug.	1	Americans burn barracks at York.
"	3	American squadron returns to Niagara.
"	7	British squadron appears off Niagara. General Porter crosses below Fort Erie.
"	8	Two American schooners upset in a squall.
"	10	Yeo captures the *Julia* and *Growler.*
"	13	Yeo lands stores at the Four-Mile Creek. Skirmish near the Cross Roads.
"	14	General Porter and Major Chapin arrive at Fort George with 364 volunteers and Indians.
"	16	Skirmish at Ball's farm. British Indians defeated.
"	17	American Indians defeated at the same place.
"	21	Sir George Prevost arrives in the British camp.
"	24	Reconnoissance in force of the American works.
"	27	British squadron appears off Niagara.
"	29	Yeo lands reinforcements at Four-Mile Creek.
Sept.	3	American fleet enters the river.
"	4	General Wilkinson takes command of the American army.
"	6	Skirmish at Ball's farm.
"	7-9	The fleets manœuvre off the mouth of the river.
"	10	Wilkinson issues an address to the Indians.
"	11	Naval action off the Genesee.
"	14	Chapin lands at Sugar Loaf.
"	17	Porter lands near Fort Erie.
"	19	A fleet of American transports arrives at Niagara.
"	23	Chauncey's fleet arrives at Niagara.
"	28	Naval engagement. The British squadron driven to Burlington.
Oct.	1	Chauncey returns.
"	2	Wilkinson sails for Sackett's Harbor with 4000 men.
"	6	Skirmish. Chapin's volunteers driven in by the Royal Scots.
"	9	The British army begins its retreat to Burlington. End of the blockade.

NIAGARA HISTORICAL SOCIETY.

Its objects are: The encouragement of the study of Canadian history and literature, the collection and preservation of Canadian historical relics, the building up of Canadian loyalty and patriotism, and the preservation of all historical landmarks in this vicinity.

Each member shall pay an annual fee of fifty cents.

The annual celebration shall be held on the 17th of September in each year.

The society shall hold eight regular meetings during the year. These meetings shall be held on the second Thursday of the month.

The annual meeting to be held on October 13th.

OFFICERS—1897-8.

Patron—WM. KIRBY, F. R. C. S.
President—MISS CARNOCHAN.
Vice-President—HENRY PAFFARD.
Secretary—ALFRED BALL.
Treasurer—MRS. A. SERVOS.
Curator—CAPT. WILKINSON.

Committee.

REV. J. C. GARRETT,
W. F. SEYMOUR, B. A.,
JNO. D. SERVOS,
MRS. ASCHER,
MISS CLEMENT.

Hon. Vice-Presidents.

PETER WHITMORE,
MRS. ROE,
CHAS. A. F. BALL.

Honorary Members.

DR. SCADDING,   MAJOR CRUIKSHANK,
REV. CANON BULL,   CAPT. M. KONKLE,
WM. GIBSON, M. P., R. O. KONKLE,
       MAJOR HISCOTT, M. P. P.

www.ingramcontent.com/pod-product-compliance
Lightning Source LLC
Chambersburg PA
CBHW020313090426

42735CB00009B/1327